To my husband and daughters,
who keep me balanced

CONTENTS

ACKNOWLEDGMENTS

MY HUSBAND AND I are equal partners in our marriage, including in the parenting of our children. My husband is also a partner in my writing business—he provides love, support, and inspiration for the work I do. So first I must thank my husband, Bill Behre.

Another important person in this equation is my book agent, Linda Konner, who helped gently shape *The Balanced Bride* from an idea scrawled on paper—and discussed in her living room a few years ago—to a full-blown proposal that was exceptionally well packaged. Thank you, Linda, for standing behind this book and believing in it, even when some publishers didn't.

Furthermore, thank you to my editor at Contemporary Books, Betsy Lancefield Lane, a recent bride herself. I believe that, because she was in that unique prewedding state of mind, Betsy saw the value and promise of this book's premise. Additionally, I am so thankful to be able to work with Betsy on yet another book project, our third.

Finally, thank you to all the balanced brides, as well as the experts, out there whose shared stories, experiences, and advice were critical to this book's real-life view. I found you through friends and family members and services such as ProfNet, MediaMap, Compu-Serve's MediaPro Forum, and the American Society of Journalists and Authors' listserve on Yahoo! Groups. Therefore, I must send a big thank-you out to each of these services for the help they provided me in researching and writing this book.

INTRODUCTION

WHAT IS *THE*
BALANCED BRIDE?

I'VE BEEN WRITING and speaking about weddings since 1994. In that time I've authored three wedding books; written hundreds of articles for magazines, newspapers, and websites; and spoken about the topic on television and radio and in Internet chats. Much of what I've covered has been logistical: how to find a dress that fits your budget, where to hold a reception, what flowers to choose for your ceremony. Although this sort of nuts-and-bolts information is important and critical to wedding planning, I've come to realize that there is a big part of the wedding picture missing from today's wedding-book offerings.

So often the bride *as a person* gets lost in the wedding-planning process. She is so busy trying to find the perfect dress for her brides-maids to wear or attempting to create the ultimate menu that she forgets to stop and take care of herself. She forgets to eat a healthy diet, get a full night's sleep, even to address any concerns or questions she has about the new adventure—marriage—upon which she's about to embark. Basically, she stops treating herself as a whole person and lets her wedding take over her life.

To help you, the bride, regain focus in your life as you plan your wedding, I've written *The Balanced Bride: Preparing Your Mind, Body, and Spirit for Your Wedding and Beyond*. This book's premise is simple and borrowed from the theory behind holistic medicine: treat the *whole person* in body, mind, and spirit, and you'll end up with a healthier, more balanced human being. In fact, the American Holistic Medical Association (AHMA) defines holistic medicine as "the art and science of healing that addresses the whole person—body, mind, and spirit." Medical studies have shown time and time again that if you neglect one at the expense of the others, you cannot be a healthy, happy, and balanced person—that is, taking care of your body without addressing the needs of your mind and spirit, or vice versa, will leave you unbalanced physically, emotionally, and spiritually. That's not how I want you to end up on your wedding day, and that's why I've written this book.

The Balanced Bride provides a much-needed wedding resource that will help you arrive at your wedding day and move into your new life as a wife a healthier person in body, mind, and spirit. Let's step back a moment, though, and take a look at how most brides go about surviving what I call "I Do Disease"—the sickness that overcomes women as they plan their weddings.

The "I Do Disease"

It's terribly sad how most brides end up feeling as their weddings approach. Instead of being thrilled that the culmination of all their hard work will finally come to fruition—and that they'll get to walk down the aisle to marry the man of their dreams—the opposite happens: most brides today find themselves becoming more and more stressed as their weddings approach. That's because most women succumb to "I Do Disease." They have allowed their weddings to infect them like some virus, leaving them little time to think about much else that is going on in their lives or to function as whole persons. I believe that the typical bride arrives at her wedding day and walks down the aisle on nervous energy—and not much else. That's because in the days, weeks, and months before the big day, she has survived on little food, sleep, and much-needed downtime.

And then there is her relationship with her future husband, which is probably being shoved to the side along with her eight hours of sleep and balanced meals. Yes, planning a wedding takes a lot of hard work, but so does maintaining a relationship. If you don't nurture your relationship as you plan your wedding, it can seriously affect your ability to have a happy marriage.

Consider this: based on conversations I've had with hundreds of brides, and interviews I've done with experts in various professions, I've determined that the state of harmony (or disharmony) in which a couple manages to get through their wedding is indicative of how successful their marriage will be. Healthy marriages happen when the husband and wife keep the lines of communication open, learn to compromise, find time to have fun together, and just genuinely enjoy themselves from the time they get engaged to the day they say, "I do." Because of their willingness to nurture their relationship as they plan their wedding, they enter marriage in a stronger state than most, and that strength will help them weather any tough times to come. If a couple puts themselves second and lets the wedding take over their lives, they are going to find themselves married to a person they may no longer know or understand. How sad.

As I mentioned earlier, it is all too common for a bride to become so consumed by the phenomenon of planning a wedding that she puts her own personal needs second and her wedding first. Take Carol as an example.

A smart, well-educated professional woman in her mid-twenties, Carol became engaged to Bob, her college sweetheart, just after Christmas not too many years ago. Carol and Bob decided to get married a little less than a year later, when the fall foliage would be brilliant in their New England town just outside Boston.

After weeks of shopping for dresses, deejays, and dessert menus, Carol was exhausted and stressed out beyond belief. Even though she and Bob lived together, they rarely saw each other (except when saying good night at bedtime). And when they did see each other, they were constantly bickering over the wedding. Who should be on the guest list? Why does your niece have to be a flower girl? What kind of officiant will we have at the wedding—a Catholic priest or a Protestant minister? Carol found it increasingly difficult to sleep at night because her thoughts were consumed with all the things she still had to do for her wedding—and all the issues that were still unresolved between her and Bob. During the day, Carol had such a knot in her stomach that she couldn't eat. Any free time she had at work or on the weekends was spent on something related to the wedding. Suddenly, it was Labor Day, and her wedding was only a few weeks away. She and Bob weren't talking, Carol's skin was a mess because of all of the stress she was under, and there was a nagging feeling in her gut that maybe, just maybe, she ought to postpone her wedding. Without even realizing it, Carol had fallen victim to "I Do Disease." She knew that if she didn't change how things were going between her and Bob, she would never be able to make that walk down the aisle.

Taking Stock

One morning, Carol decided she had to do something. She stopped Bob on his way to the shower and asked if they could talk when he got out. He was so surprised by her request that he sat right down on the bed in his pajamas. Carol started by telling Bob that she loved him very much, but she was having doubts about the wedding. It wasn't that she didn't want to marry him, but she was so stressed out from all the plans that she felt like the two had grown apart. After a long silence, Bob admitted he was feeling the same.

The two talked about all that had happened in their lives since they'd gotten engaged at Christmas and how amazed they were that their wedding was only a few weeks away. Then, they started reminiscing about college and the fun things they used to do before they had a wedding to worry about, and they realized that life together had stopped being enjoyable. But they also knew that it wasn't too late.

Carol suggested that after work that day, they order in takeout food and then, over dinner, compare notes as to where they actually were in finalizing their wedding. This would help to put everything wedding-related in perspective and, more importantly, give them some time together. Each went off to work in a better mood than they had in weeks, let alone months.

That evening, Carol and Bob did as they said. They figured out that the wedding was further along than they'd realized. But something even more important happened: Carol and Bob had taken time to nurture their relationship. Sure, it wasn't anything sexy — just takeout food eaten on paper plates — but it helped them feel connected again and, in turn, made them feel less stressed out. That evening, Carol and Bob decided that they needed to have a date twice a week for dinner, and that dinner date would have to become a priority in their crazy lives. This quiet time together before the wedding ended up setting an important precedent that would help Carol and Bob keep their relationship strong.

In addition, Carol decided that she needed to start taking better care of her body if she wanted to look her best on her wedding day. With only a few weeks until the event, she didn't have much time, but she also wasn't going to let a deadline stand in her way. The next day, she called her physician for a referral to a nutritionist. Then, she called a local spa and bought herself a gift—a facial and six massages over the next six weeks. Furthermore, Carol started taking some time for herself during her lunch hour. Instead of spending the entire hour doing things for her wedding, she spent only thirty minutes writing wedding-related E-mails and making calls. During the remaining thirty minutes, she took a walk, which gave her a much-needed breath of fresh air and a chance to clear her head. Bob also started taking care of himself by getting up early three days a week to run.

A Happy Ending—and a New Beginning

Carol and Bob were able to work out all of their unresolved issues and go on to have a wonderful wedding. During the ceremony and reception, they both looked refreshed and relaxed and truly in love (which they are). Thanks to improved eating habits and better stress management, Carol's skin cleared up, and she was a radiant bride. Their ceremony went off without a hitch, the food at the reception was divine, and all the guests loved the swing band. Their wedding was one that they both could look back fondly on—mostly because the two of them had recognized early enough that if they didn't take care of themselves and their relationship, there probably wouldn't have been a wedding at all.

Now, two years later, Carol and Bob continue to have a dinner date twice a week, as they did when they were engaged. It gives them much-needed time to reconnect as a couple and allows them time-out time from their stressful jobs. Who knows where Carol and Bob may have ended up had they not made the effort before their wedding to get back together in mind, body, and spirit? It may not have been such a picture-perfect ending.

Carol and Bob's story shows why it is important to take care of your whole self (including your relationship) while you are planning your wedding. Not only does becoming the balanced bride help you be healthy, happy, and wise on your wedding day and beyond, but it will also give you the physical, mental, and spiritual strength to embark on this new adventure called marriage.

Making *The Balanced Bride* Work for You

Believe me: in my years of writing about weddings and working as a wedding expert, I've met or interviewed hundreds of brides who've let their personal lives play second fiddle to their weddings, and their personal, psychological, and relationship health suffered because of it. Many of them faced tough times after the wedding as they attempted to navigate their new territory as husband and wife. Many brides have told me that they wished they'd known ahead of time how much stress the wedding would put on their relationship with each other. That's how I conceived of *The Balanced Bride*.

I believe *The Balanced Bride* will give you a new set of tools in a way that no other wedding book does. It will help you learn how you can obtain optimal physical, mental, and spiritual health; have the energy to plan the wedding of your dreams; and go on to live a happy and healthy life with the man you love.

Like holistic medicine, *The Balanced Bride* approaches your pre- and postwedding health in three ways: body, mind, and spirit. You'll notice that the book is divided into three sections representing each of these parts of you. Within each section are chapters related to the topic.

For example, in the "Body" section, I offer advice on eating well for sustained energy, learning to love your body, and the importance of having a regular physical. Within "Mind," you'll learn why it's critical to take time to pamper yourself regularly (a lesson Carol learned) and how you can balance all the elements in your life—from family and friends to careers and kids. And in the "Spirit" section, I help you discover how you and your future husband can become soul mates (if you aren't already), plus I provide guidelines for planning a wedding ceremony on a spiritual level that's right for you both.

Obviously, you are committed to your partner—after all, you've agreed to marry him. Let me help you take care of yourself in a way that will allow you to stay madly in love and feel great as you walk down the aisle. I'm confident you'll find *The Balanced Bride* a valuable resource as you plan your wedding—and for your new life together. Now, let's get reading.

Part I

BODY

1

THE BASICS OF GOOD NUTRITION

I COULD USE a number of analogies to describe what it's like to plan a wedding. It's like taking on a second, full-time career. It's like training to run a marathon. It's like preparing for a session of the United Nations Security Council. But what it all comes down to is this: planning your wedding requires an extraordinary amount of time, energy, and thought, and you simply won't be able to do it well if you're overtired, undernourished, and out of shape. That's why putting the care of your body at the top of your wedding to-do list will help you arrive at your wedding day a happier, healthier bride.

One of the fundamentals of being a happier and healthier bride is eating right. I'm not talking about eating to lose weight but basically treating your body right by giving it healthy doses of healthy food. I'm sure like every other person on the planet you're aware that you should be eating more whole grains, fruits, and vegetables and less fats, sugars, and processed foods. Yes, I'm sure you know this. But are you actually following this good advice? Probably not, because most of your contemporaries aren't following it either. But let me tell you why you should be.

"People think that they should automatically know how to eat well, and that's not always the case," says Dominique Adair, M.S., a registered dietitian and nutrition programs coordinator at New York Sports Club in New York City. What complicates this issue for most women is a lifetime spent dieting or time spent following fad diets that say carbohydrates are bad and protein is good, or cabbage soup is all you can eat for days at a time.

"Any eating plan that is of short duration or so different from a normal way of life, such as one where one food group is excluded in favor of another, not only sets you up for nutritional risks but guarantees that you'll gain weight once you resume your traditional eating habits," warns Robyn Flipse, a registered dietitian and coauthor of *The Wedding Dress Diet* (Doubleday, 2000), a book that focuses on healthy eating for the wedding and beyond.

THE ESSENTIALS OF HEALTHY EATING

To help you get a handle on what comprises a healthy diet, let's turn to the Food Guide Pyramid from the U.S. Department of Agriculture (USDA). (If you'd like to print a copy of the Pyramid to carry with you, visit the website at nal.usda.gov/fnic/fpyr/pyramid.html.) This pyramid provides an easy-to-understand outline of balanced food choices and serving sizes for every meal and every snack you eat each day. Why a pyramid? The idea is that at the base of the pyramid, you'll find a concentration of lower-fat, healthier foods, like grains, fruits, and vegetables, that you should eat more of on a daily basis. Toward the top are the foods you should eat less of, like fats, oils, and sweets.

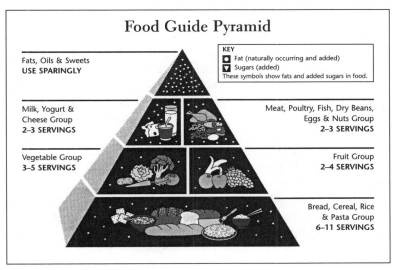

Food Guide Pyramid

KEY
- ◻ Fat (naturally occurring and added)
- ▼ Sugars (added)

These symbols show fats and added sugars in food.

Fats, Oils & Sweets
USE SPARINGLY

Milk, Yogurt &
Cheese Group
2–3 SERVINGS

Meat, Poultry, Fish, Dry Beans,
Eggs & Nuts Group
2–3 SERVINGS

Vegetable Group
3–5 SERVINGS

Fruit Group
2–4 SERVINGS

Bread, Cereal, Rice
& Pasta Group
6–11 SERVINGS

U.S. Department of Agriculture and U.S. Department of Health and Human Services

While the Pyramid tells you which food groups to make choices from, you may wonder what constitutes a serving. Here are examples from each food group:

- A slice of bread equals one serving of grains.
- A medium-sized banana equals one serving of fruit.
- A half cup of baby carrots equals one serving of vegetables.
- One cup of milk or yogurt equals one serving of dairy.
- Two tablespoons of peanut butter equal one serving of a protein-rich food.

Now that you know *what* you should be eating, *how* are you going to make this work for you? Simple: get extra help.

"Just as you would go out and seek the advice of a caterer or a florist for your wedding, why not take the time and invest a little money in making sure your physical and nutritional state is in optimal condition for your wedding?" suggests Adair. And the expert who can give you the tools to accomplish this healthy-eating task is a registered dietitian, like Adair. (To find a registered dietitian, contact the American Dietetic Association, which offers a referral service. Check out the association's website at eatright.org.)

What can you expect from meeting with a registered dietitian? First, she'll probably explain that your idea of healthy eating needs to be a lifelong approach, not a one-fix wonder. You can't just click your heels and have a healthier diet. It *will* take some work on your part, but your registered dietitian should be reasonable about her expectations of what you can accomplish as you plan your wedding. "It shouldn't be an all-or-nothing approach," says Adair. "I realize that I'm not going to make nutrition a top priority with a busy bride, but we can figure out ways to work it into her to-do list." Adds Flipse, "You don't want to make up eating rules that will make her feel even more confined."

> ### Wedding Wisdom
> *I had wanted to lose weight, and my engagement was the push I needed to get serious. I started working with a personal trainer, changed my diet, and was able to tone up and slim down in time for my wedding. Looking back on the wedding day, I felt like the perfect, beautiful bride. I felt so good in my clothes that it was an inspiration to keep the weight off, which I have.*
> —Melissa, Pennsylvania

Because there will be a lot of back and forth as you figure out what works best for you as you try to eat healthy, you should plan to have a few visits with the registered dietitian. In one of the first visits, expect to get a quick lesson on the Food Guide Pyramid, plus an assessment of your current eating habits. The registered dietitian may also ask about past eating successes and failures so she can figure out the easiest way to get you to eat a healthier diet without stressing you out too much. She may also send you away with some homework, such as trying your hand at keeping a food log.

THE FOOD LOG

"When it comes to food and what you've eaten, people don't have good memories," says Flipse, "and they will rationalize things that play in their favor." As crazy as it seems, people often believe that food eaten on the run or off someone else's plate simply doesn't count in their daily calorie count. But it is this kind of all-day eating that can easily send you down the road of poor nutrition. It's what also leads to unwanted weight gain. "If we were better monitors of our dietary intakes, there would be no obesity and no one would put on weight each year," adds Flipse.

This is where the food log comes in: by committing to writing down everything you eat, you'll quickly become aware of how much you actually eat every day—and that will have a powerful effect on your ability to change your behavior to eat better. "If you are writing your food intake down, it will tell you that you can't go get another Tootsie Roll off your secretary's desk because you've already had five today," says Flipse. "If you don't write that down, you'll justify eating more candy by saying, 'Oh it's just one more Tootsie Roll' instead of owning up to the fact that you've already eaten five of them."

> **Wedding Wisdom**
> *I joined a Weight Watchers at-work program about eight months before the wedding. Meeting once a week, weighing in, and talking to the rest of the group was a huge inspiration to get in shape by my wedding day, which I did.*
> JANE, MASSACHUSETTS

Your registered dietitian may ask that you keep a food log for a week, at which point she'll review what you're eating—and what you're not. (By the way, a food log can be as simple as notations in the margins of your daily planner or as elaborate as a notebook that you'll use exclusively to write down your eating habits. The choice is yours.) Don't try to change your eating habits during this first week of keeping a food log to "please" your registered dietitian. Simply record all the food and beverages that go into your mouth so that, upon reviewing your eating habits, the registered dietitian can identify any food patterns or nutritional deficiencies. "Sometimes you

Drink Up

Most people don't realize that they spend a good part of their daily lives dehydrated. That's because most aren't getting their recommended sixty-four ounces of water each day—more if you're exercising and sweating on a regular basis. In fact, a recent study shows that 50 percent of people *know* they don't drink enough water, yet the average American drinks only thirty-six ounces of water each day—just a bit more than half of the recommended daily amount. Sometimes we mistake thirst for hunger or exhaustion. So, the next time you're looking for a cup of coffee or a doughnut to give you a three-o'clock boost, have eight ounces of water instead. Chances are that after you've had your drink, you'll feel a lot better and less like eating or having coffee.

discover that a person is missing whole food groups," says Flipse. Sometimes, however, the log helps uncover good eating habits you may not even be aware of, such as the fact that you eat enough grains or are good about getting your sixty-four ounces of water every day.

Menu Planning

Keeping a food log will probably become a big part of your transition to healthy eating. Not only will it record what you are or are not eating and drinking, but it can also help you plan your meals for busy days. If you're going to be running to visit with the florist or the calligrapher on your lunch hour, the presence of a food log will help remind you that you need to bring something that constitutes a meal that you can eat in the car between appointments. Adds Flipse, "You've got to think ahead, because you'll always make a poor food choice when you're overly hungry or crunched for time." So, before you leave for work each day, take a few minutes and use your food log to plan that day's meals. This way you can adjust your meal plans based on how busy you might be that day. "You don't need to stash a box of granola bars in your desk or leave the house with an apple," adds Flipse, because these foods alone won't take care of all of your food and nutritional needs for the eight hours or more that you'll be away from home or take the place of a complete and balanced lunch. Instead, figure out if there is a deli that you can visit that day to order a healthy lunch. Or decide whether you should spend time that morning making your lunch and packing a few extra snacks. Write down in your food log whatever you've chosen, and check it off as you go along. Then, at the end of the day, you can review how well— or poorly—you've eaten. This information will help you figure out an optimal choice for dinner. For example, were you low on vegetables throughout the day? Then you might want to make a vegetable stir-fry that night. Or are you missing some servings of dairy? Then an egg-white omelet with low-fat cheese is in order.

When it comes to overall menu planning, how you do it is entirely up to you. Some people like the structure and guidance of sample menus, and if you're one of them, then ask your registered dietitian to come up with a few days' worth of menus, including breakfast, lunch, dinner, and snacks that you can use. Others like to be more in control and create their own menus. "In my opinion, the easiest diet to stick to is one you wrote yourself," says Flipse. "If you've read that you're supposed to eat three black olives and tuna

Potable Portables

Buying bottle after bottle of spring water can add up monetarily, not to mention fill your recycling bin, but drinking bottled water is a great way to stay hydrated. Here's a way to have the filtered water you like and the fluids that your body needs, plus save money and the environment: invest in a Fill & Go Water Filtration Bottle from Brita. This reusable plastic sports bottle has a drop-in replaceable carbon filter (much like the popular Brita pitchers) and a push-up spout for easy drinking. Just fill the bottle from the tap, let the water filter through, and you've got great tasting water on the go. The bottle costs about $7.99 and is available at mass merchandise, food, drug, and department specialty stores.

for lunch, but you don't like black olives and aren't in the mood for fish, then how can you follow that plan?"

Of course, a sensible registered dietitian would never write a sample menu containing foods you don't like, so if you go the preplanned menu route, make sure you make any food aversions clear so you don't feel restricted by her suggestions—thus setting yourself up for failure. Also, work with your registered dietitian to help uncover foods you've eaten in the past or "tricks" you've used before that have helped you feel better and eat healthier. "The more foods you can come up with spontaneously, the easier the menus are to follow," says Adair. So, if you remember that last summer you felt really great when you ate a grapefruit with breakfast each morning, kept cut-up watermelon in the fridge for easy snacking, and loved drinking iced herbal teas on a regular basis, figure out ways to work these into your new and improved way of eating.

> **Wedding Wisdom**
> *I maintained my workout schedule, taking cardio-karate kickboxing classes to strengthen my arms (sleeveless dress, July wedding) and manage stress. I also made sure to eat better, focusing on complex carbohydrates, proteins, and fruits and vegetables for snacks (in lieu of sweets).*
> JUDY, NEW JERSEY

Here are some additional tricks the registered dietitian may suggest you try to help keep your eating on course:

- Stock up on single-serving healthy foods that make meal planning a snap, such as always having cups of yogurt in the refrigerator.

- Take advantage of your supermarket's prepackaged salads and fruits, which are washed and ready to eat.

- Look to frozen foods like veggie burgers and "fake" chicken nuggets (made from soy products instead of meat) as healthy protein alternatives. Best of all, they are ready to eat after just a few minutes in the microwave oven.

• Keep bottled water on hand at all times, and try to carry a bottle with you when you're out and about. If the water is nearby, it will be easier to get your recommended sixty-four ounces of fluid each day. Also remember that noncaffeine beverages, like herbal tea, seltzer, and caffeine-free soda, as well as soup and milk, all count toward your daily requirement of at least sixty-four ounces of liquid.

• Always go food shopping with a list in hand, and never go when you're hungry. That's when you're most likely to go on a buying binge. Although shopping on the perimeter of a supermarket is always a good idea—it's where you find the freshest, least-processed foods, like fruits, vegetables, and dairy—don't limit yourself to this area of the supermarket. Good food choices can be found in the inner aisles, as well. Here is where you'll find such staples as whole-grain breads, rice, beans, and jars of salsa. Just try not to linger in the cookie aisle, where you may be tempted by food you may regret buying and eating later.

• Don't have food in the house for which you know you have a weakness and that you're trying to cut down on eating. "I know a bride-to-be who was constantly buying chocolate candy in case people came over," says Adair, "and I told her, 'No, you're buying them because *you* want them. Your guests can eat baby carrots.' It's so easy to say that you're buying them for someone else when you really want them for yourself." So, if you have a weakness for cheese and crackers, don't serve them when you invite a photographer over to look at his book. The photographer will be just as happy eating raw vegetables and low-fat dip, and so will you, in case you decide to join him in snacking.

In addition, if you tend to eat when you're bored or stressed out, you'll be less likely to binge if there is nothing in the house to binge on. "If you open the refrigerator because you want to soothe yourself with food and you don't find the food you want, you tend to stop and ask yourself, 'Am I really hungry?'" says Flipse. If you aren't, then you won't eat. But if you are, you'll go for the more healthy

Hints on Hydration

To make getting your minimum sixty-four ounces of water easier, try to carry a sports bottle or bottle of water with you each day, drinking as you go. For example, I keep a sixteen-ounce bottle of water on my desk at work, in the car with me, or in my bag when I travel. I know that to get enough water, I must drink and refill the bottle at least four times throughout the day—more if I've been exercising or it's hot outside. I mark down in my food log each time I've gone through sixteen ounces of water, which keeps me on track for staying hydrated. Here's another method to consider: registered dietitian Dominique Adair once had a client for whom lining up eight eight-ounce glasses of water on her kitchen counter was a great way to make sure she drank sufficient water each day. "She could put one glass into the dishwasher each time she drank its contents," says Adair, "and if she got to the end of the day and had two glasses left, then she knew she needed to drink that leftover water before she went to bed."

options you have in stock, like oranges or carrots, rather than cookies and ice cream. And eating the former rather than the latter will leave you feeling a lot better, both physically and psychologically, in the end.

EATING WELL WHEN EATING OUT

It's likely that during the wedding-planning period, you're going to spend many evenings eating out—because someone is taking you out to celebrate your engagement, you're having dinner at a restaurant you're considering using for your reception, or you simply don't feel like cooking dinner that night. With eating better as one of your missions, you're going to have to do some reconnaissance work before you visit any restaurant, and then be careful about the food choices you make once you're there. In addition, these eating-out nights are the perfect times to use your food log to do meal planning in advance so that you don't finish dinner feeling guilty that you ate way more than you wanted.

First, when being taken out to dinner, don't be afraid to find out ahead of time where you're going to eat. That way you can call ahead and get a preview of the menu. This will better prepare you for the meal that lies ahead and help you make food choices throughout the day. If you know, for example, that you're going to a place that doesn't offer a lot of fresh fruit and vegetable options, you'll need to make sure you get your fruit and vegetable servings at breakfast and lunch and with your snacks. Conversely, if you're going to a restaurant that is known for its overflowing salads and fabulous fish dishes, you know that you'll be able to take care of your vegetable and protein requirements adequately at dinner.

High-Energy Snacking

One of the ways to avoid getting famished and turning to a box of Girl Scout cookies for a quick pick-me-up is to plan for and eat high-energy snacks throughout the day. What do I mean by a high-energy snack? One that is nutritionally sound, will satisfy your hunger, and will give you the energy you need to get your work done and not arrive at your next meal fully famished. The best way to accomplish this is to choose a snack with a combination of nutrients—some carbohydrates, protein, and fat. "It's like a time-release cold capsule," says registered dietitian Dominique Adair. That is, your body digests carbohydrates the fastest, then protein, and then, finally, it digests fats the slowest. So, if you have a snack with each of these components, it will leave you feeling fuller longer and having more energy. The following snacks encompass all three nutrients:

- A teaspoon of peanut butter with a banana
- Low-fat cheese with crackers
- A cup of low-fat fruit yogurt
- Turkey in a whole-wheat pita

Furthermore, meal replacement products like Slim-Fast bars or milk-based smoothies taste great, are high in calcium, and include all the nutrients of a high-energy snack: carbohydrates, protein, and fat.

Second, for wedding-planning meals, such as when you're going to taste a caterer's menu, go with reinforcements. That is, along with your fiancé, bring a few friends or family members whose opinions you trust and who will be willing to eat food with you so you won't feel responsible for eating everything that the caterer brings out. This is especially helpful with a caterer who will be serving a full range of desserts. Also, let the caterer know ahead of time that although you're interested in seeing what he has to offer in traditional wedding fare, which your friends can help you taste, you're also interested in sampling his healthier menu options, such as salmon and sautéed vegetables.

> **Wedding Wisdom**
> *It is eight months until the wedding, and I just joined a gym and started to eat healthier. No more fast food. It is not about losing weight, but about being fit and healthy. I will have a husband and, in the future, a family to pass eating habits on to. It is important for me to provide a good example.*
> MELISSA, IOWA

Third, try not to attend food- and wedding-related meetings on an empty stomach. If you find yourself at a bar at seven o'clock listening to a band and you haven't eaten since lunch, chances are you're going to wolf down peanuts, chips, and beer to fill up. Likewise, it will be less tempting to eat your way through the caterer's Viennese table of desserts on a full stomach. Plan ahead for these events and stock up on healthy snacks that you can eat and fill up on beforehand.

Fourth, on the nights when you don't feel like cooking, don't allow yourself to end up in a fast-food joint or a restaurant where there's a limited menu. Instead, head for a restaurant where you'll have some leeway for making healthier food substitutions. "Even at a place like a diner you can get sliced tomatoes on your salad or order a dinner of soup and sandwich rather than just going with a burger," says Flipse.

Finally, remember that ultimately you are in control of what and how much you eat. Just because you're presented with a huge bowl of pasta (which probably comprises two or three servings, not one, by the way) that doesn't mean you have to eat the whole thing. Remind yourself that the clean-plate club, of which your mother or father may have been president and chief executive officer, is a thing of the past. "The most common job that people fail at is estimating how much they need to eat," says Flipse, who recommends working on reconnecting with the feeling of being satisfied when you eat. Way too many people eat to the point of being stuffed rather than listening to their bodies, which means knowing when to stop eating before you feel too full.

In addition, you need to give yourself permission to eat different amounts of food on different days and at different meals. That's because sometimes you are simply more or less hungry than at other times. If one night you eat an entire bowl of ravioli before you feel satisfied, but the next time you visit that restaurant you only feel like eating four raviolis, that's OK. Also, if you know you have a weakness for all-you-can-eat buffets, don't go to restaurants that offer them. And it's always OK to take food home with you. So, if you find yourself at a restaurant and you don't want to eat any more of your entrée, simply ask the waiter to take the food away and wrap it up so you can take it home. Once the plate is gone, you can't pick at it.

THE WEDDING EATING PLAN

With all that you've learned about healthy eating, you may be worried that you're going to blow it on the big day. Well, don't worry, because if you've approached this healthier eating plan as a lifelong lifestyle change, it will carry you through to your wedding day and beyond. Thanks to weeks and months of making healthy food choices, you'll almost know instinctively what's the best thing for you to eat at your wedding and what you should only taste. And let me let you in on a little secret from a bride who has been there: if anything is going to happen on your wedding day, it's going to be that you'll be too busy greeting guests and dancing with your new husband to remember to eat. (At my wedding, my caterer chased me around with a plate of food, asking that I eat a little something!) And I'm not saying that's a good thing. Because a wedding day is a veritable marathon event, if you don't eat, you're not going to be feeling and looking your best throughout the day. That's why I suggest you set up the following two food-related plans for the big day.

One, identify a friend or family member who will be your designated "feeder." This person's job is simply to make sure that you eat before the ceremony and at the wedding so you don't run out of energy or, worse yet, end up downing two glasses of champagne on

---

Wedding Wisdom

I have become much healthier since getting engaged. I began by reading more about health, nutrition, and exercise. In fact, instead of subscribing to all the bridal magazines, I started getting magazines for a healthier lifestyle. I began putting more thought into what I cooked and ate. And, though I do have the goal of looking my best at my wedding to motivate me, these healthy habits will also serve me well for the rest of my life. I have also gotten my fiancé on a health kick, just because I am more active and improving my own eating habits. For example, our date night used to consist of a heavy meal and a movie; now it is a long walk, finished with a sushi dinner.

SARAH, ILLINOIS

an empty stomach. Decide ahead of time what you want to eat before the ceremony. Be sure you choose a favorite food that you'll be able to eat (despite the butterflies in your stomach), is seemingly nutritious, and won't give you heartburn or bad breath or, worse, make you gassy. (Stay away from beans and broccoli!) Now is not the time to turn to leftover Chinese food or pizza as your wedding-day nutrition staple.

And, two, when your designated "feeder" suggests you eat, listen to him or her, like I did with the caterer at my wedding. Don't say, "Oh, I'm not hungry right now," because you probably won't feel hungry at all that day, but you will be. With all of the things you'll have on your mind, like getting married, you're probably going to feel a little nervous, so you may not want to eat. But eating will actually calm the butterflies and chase away any feelings of nausea, which are completely normal with such a high level of excitement. So, before you walk down the aisle, have a small meal. Then, at your reception, have a bite or two of the menu you worked so hard to plan. Doing both will give you the energy you need to enjoy your wedding day.

THE HONEYMOON EATING PLAN

Now, as far as your honeymoon goes, certainly you should relax, enjoy yourself, and eat and drink whatever you want—but within reason. Remember: your plan to eat healthier is a lifelong decision—not one that says vacations and honeymoons don't apply. "The pressure is probably off, the dress is in the closet or at the dry cleaner, and the worst thing that can come of that is that you spend your honeymoon eating and drinking excessively," says Flipse. Do you really want to come back from your honeymoon feeling bloated and having gained a few pounds? "Remember, this is the person you're going to be sharing meals with for the rest of your life, and there's no reason to turn your honeymoon into a food orgy," she adds. So although it's perfectly OK to indulge in some of the delicious desserts at the resort or have an after-dinner drink on a couple of nights, try to do so in moderation. Instead of each ordering the mouthwatering truffles for dessert, why not split a plate of them instead? "Eating a whole slice of cheesecake instead of just a little doesn't make it taste better," says Flipse.

Also, if you're honeymooning in a tropical locale where it's safe to eat fresh fruit, and the fish at dinner was just swimming in the ocean earlier that day, take advantage of this abundance of healthier food options as you choose your meals. This way you can attempt to expand your healthier eating palette and make doing so a part of the adventure of your honeymoon. By continuing to make good food choices on your honeymoon and beyond, you'll wake up each day of your married life looking and feeling great.

BALANCE: THE BOTTOM LINE

Your mother couldn't have said it better: if you don't eat healthy foods, you won't grow up to be big and strong. Despite the Superman (or Superwoman, as it were) overtones, the same advice applies to your adult eating habits and your ability to survive your wedding. If you are spending the days, weeks, and months leading up to your wedding depriving yourself of the food and water that your body desperately needs, you are going to arrive at your wedding day a worn-out, exhausted, and possibly ill person—and an unbalanced bride. That's why I recommend getting a refresher course on good nutrition.

Here are some suggestions to keep in mind:

• Get thee to a registered dietitian for an objective overview of your current state of eating. You'll learn where you can improve your meal- and snack-time habits, or, if the case may be, pat yourself on the back for a job well done if, for example, you discover you've been good about getting enough calcium.

• Increase your intake of liquids to a minimum of sixty-four ounces a day, every day—more if you're exercising or it's hot outside. Unfortunately, thanks to our current love affair with coffee and other caffeinated beverages, we tend to walk around in a dehydrated state, which can lead to exhaustion and overeating. Drink up—water, that is!

• Create an eating-out battle plan for nights spent tasting caterers' menus and listening to bands in bars, as well as for the big day and beyond. This plan will help keep your healthy eating on track for today and the future.

All told, you should be nutritionally balanced and in tip-top shape in no time.

2

YOUR BODY,
YOUR SELF

WHEN I GOT engaged many years ago, I knew I had many tasks to complete before I could walk down the aisle and marry the man of my dreams. I needed to find a place to be married, figure out who would cater the affair, and choose what kind of entertainment we would have, among other things. In addition, I also figured I had to lose weight, a task it seems that many brides add to their already overflowing wedding to-do list.

I can't give you any logical reason for my weight-loss desire—I was at a healthy weight for me, I was eating well and exercising regularly, and, best of all, I was wearing a size ten/twelve, which is hardly overweight. But for some reason, I'd latched on to the idea that weight loss was a must-do once I began planning my wedding. Perhaps you're feeling the same way, too, but I need to ask: why?

If weight loss has been a goal of yours for some time now and your upcoming wedding is just the kick in the pants that you need to get motivated—and your doctor agrees that your body would be healthier five, ten, or twenty pounds lighter—then by all means join Weight Watchers or the gym or start meeting with a registered die-titian (R.D.) to improve your eating habits. If you think you need to lose weight for your wedding "just because," however, then I implore you to take a few minutes and investigate *why* it is that you're equat-ing a number on the scale or the dress size of the clothing you're wearing with your wedding-day bliss.

LOVE YOURSELF AS YOU ARE

One of the things I believe every bride-to-be needs to be reminded of—and this includes you—is this: your fiancé loves you for who you are inside and out, and he loves you now—not contingent upon your being twenty pounds lighter on your wedding day. (If he does, then you've got issues to work out and you probably need to seriously reconsider whether this is the person you want to spend the rest of your life with.) Chances are, the only pressure you're feeling to look different on the day you walk down the aisle is coming from inside your very own head. I know how it goes, because I once thought that way as well.

As I mentioned earlier, when I got engaged, I figured I needed to lose weight for my wedding because that seemed like what every bride-to-be does. But then a funny thing happened on a lunch-break shopping excursion that changed how I viewed my wedding-day body forever.

I'd decided to pop into a local department store and check out the latest fashions. Upon exiting the escalator, I found myself quite unexpectedly face-to-face with the wedding dress of my dreams. It was showcased along with other formal-wear dresses, which were floors away from the store's bridal boutique, but it didn't matter to me. I knew this was the perfect dress for my wedding day because it had all the elements I liked in clothing—an A-line silhouette, delicate embroidery that added just a hint of detail without overwhelming the entire ensemble, and cotton and linen fabrics, two of my favorites. Best of all, it could easily pass for a wedding dress, albeit one of a more casual nature. I grabbed dresses in sizes ten and twelve and headed for the dressing room. Although the size ten was a bit snug, the size twelve fit as if the dress were custom-made for me. It hugged me in all the right places and played up my assets while hiding my liabilities. I knew I had to have this dress, and with a less-than-$200 price tag, I didn't hesitate to buy it.

Once I paid for the dress, stepped out of the store, and headed back to work, I had an epiphany: I no longer longed to lose weight. This dress looked fabulous on me as I was, so why would I want to change my body now? Besides, any weight loss at this point would result in my having to pay for a dress alteration, something I did not want to do. Plus, there was the fact that all along my husband (then fiancé) kept telling me that he loved me as I was and didn't understand why I wanted to lose weight. It's sort of sad that it took a silly old dress to show me that he was right.

> ### Wedding Wisdom
>
> *I am learning that I like myself better when I am strong, not just when I am thin. And I know that my fiancé loves my body as it is and doesn't view a stick-thin supermodel as an ideal.*
>
> SARAH, ILLINOIS

In essence, making the commitment to wear this dress on my wedding day forced me to accept my body as it was, to live with it, and to learn to love it, and that gave me an exceptional sense of inner calm. Without the fear of weight-loss failure hanging over my head, suddenly a huge stressor in my prewedding life disappeared.

If you truly don't need to lose weight before your wedding, such as for doctor-approved health reasons, then I believe you should work on learning to love your body rather than trying to change it. Remember: you were born with a certain body type and physical traits and, short of extensive cosmetic surgery, there isn't much that you can do to alter how you look. "If you're born to stand five foot four with short limbs, you'll never have that long-legged model look," says Diane Forden, editor in chief of *Bridal Guide* magazine. "Going through life hating your body and how you look is so unhealthy. And by doing so, you'll never be happy."

One of the ways that you can work on being happy about how you look today is to start focusing on the positive and putting away your negatives. How? Sit down with your fiancé and ask him to talk about all of the things he loves about you. Hopefully, he won't find this exercise too silly to complete because I believe it will be really helpful for you and your self-esteem. Don't sit there waiting to hear things that the media has told you are important for beautiful women to have, such as six-pack abs or legs that stretch forever. Instead, focus in on exactly what he highlights about you, and take those compliments to heart. You might even go so far as to write these ideas down.

Of course, there are instances where time and distance won't allow you to ask your fiancé to pull a Romeo and do a "How do I

Wedding Wisdom

I was never into working out in a gym, but felt that I wanted to get in shape for the wedding. So I joined a gym about nine months prior to the wedding date, but quickly discovered that my preengagement habits were not to be changed. I had so many other things going on that to make another major change in my routine was just too much. Fortunately, I got some great advice from a newlywed coworker: the only parts of your body to worry about are your arms and shoulders; the rest is covered up by the big white dress!

SARA, NEW YORK

love thee? Let me count the ways" list. In this instance, I suggest spending a few moments thinking back to all of the great things he's told you about yourself, what drew him to you, and why he wants to spend the rest of his life with you.

Once you've got a list of things your fiancé loves about you, add your own "what I love about me" qualities. This task may be hard to accomplish at first—especially because we women are so plugged in to finding our flaws. So, instead of beating yourself up about all the things you want to change about yourself, think instead about the aspects of your personality that seem to draw people to you or the skills about which you're most proud. These can range from the sublime to the ridiculous, but do try to capture what's special about you and what attributes you would never change about yourself.

If I were doing this exercise with my husband, I know exactly what he'd say he loves about me—my smile and that I make him laugh. I believe these are my two best assets, and I would include them on my own list of "what I love about me" qualities. Yes, I also happen to like that my arms have some muscle definition to them and that tank tops look great on me, thanks to my weight-lifting routine, but I know that my ability to make my husband laugh will sustain our relationship longer than my buff arms will.

You've got to think the same way about yourself. Sure, it's OK to highlight some of your finer physical attributes if you must, but try to stay focused on all of the good things you bring to your relationship with your fiancé.

Once you've got some positive attributes down on paper, I suggest you either stick them on your bulletin board at work or keep them in your wallet. That way, when you're doubting yourself or

> ### Wedding Wisdom
> *My dress has a high neckline with a low back. Everyone tells me I have a good back—and that's what the audience is going to see when I'm up at the altar—so why not show it off?*
>
> Michelle,
> Massachusetts

thinking that losing five pounds will fix everything in your life or calm the chaos surrounding your wedding, you can get a quick reality check by reflecting on what is truly important—what makes you lovable and why your fiancé wants to marry you.

Finding a Dress That Flatters

Now that you're on track to start loving yourself as you are, let's face reality: you've got a dress to buy for your wedding, and regardless of how much you weigh or what size dress you wear, you need to figure out how to find a dress that flatters. Doing so actually may be easier than you think. Here are some tips to get you going.

Keep Your Regular Wardrobe in Mind

> **Wedding Wisdom**
>
> *I hired a dressmaker to design and custom-make my champagne-pink, sleeveless dress with a detachable French lace train, matching handbag, and bolero jacket from the leftover fabric. Not only was the dress gorgeous, I actually wore it again (without the train and with different "nonwedding" shoes) to a black-tie event a few months later!*
>
> Judy, New Jersey

For starters, just because this is your wedding dress, that doesn't mean you can't follow your personal fashion dos and don'ts. In fact, you should. Say you're a woman with a pear-shaped body and an ample lower half. You would never buy a career dress with a heavily detailed skirt that flounced out at the hips because you know that this is not a style that flatters you. Similarly, you would be wise to steer clear of a wedding dress with such features. Instead, think about the kinds of clothing you already have in your closet and use these as your guide to good wedding-dress choices. Do you favor dresses or suits with slim silhouettes? If so, then stick to these kinds of wedding-dress choices when you go shopping.

Work with Your Body Type

When Chicago bride-to-be Michelle was looking for her wedding gown, she dreamed of a dress with a fluffy, white tulle skirt. Once she started shopping, however, she discovered that all of the dresses with this kind of skirt also featured big bodices that overtook her petite five-feet one-inch frame. Every dress Michelle tried on just swallowed her up. She realized that to balance her small size and keep true to her dream of a dress with a big skirt, Michelle needed to look for a slightly different silhouette. She found it in a strapless gown that she tried on by chance at a trunk show. It was the perfect combination—and the perfect dress. "Because I am small, showing my shoulders and arms made the difference," Michelle says, and this allowed her to stand out in the gown—rather than be overwhelmed by it.

According to Forden of *Bridal Guide*, Michelle combined the right elements in her gown. "If you're petite, you don't want a dress that has too many details, such as a very voluminous skirt and a lot going on in the bodice," she says. "If you go for details on the top, you should choose a plainer skirt on the bottom." Or, in the case of Michelle, the opposite ended up being true.

Go Shopping with an Open Mind

Even if you've done everything right in shopping for your wedding gown—kept your wardrobe in mind and looked for dresses that work with your assets—sometimes you end up finding your dream dress

> **Wedding Wisdom**
>
> *I'm short and slim, so I heeded the experts' advice and bought an A-line gown with princess seams, to give the illusion of height. I also avoided elaborate embellishments that would overwhelm my frame, like lace, tulle, and beading.*
>
> KARISA, CALIFORNIA

where and when you least expect it. Adds Forden, "Sometimes you may think a dress you see in a magazine is the perfect one, but another entirely is the one that wins your heart."

Take Carla, a Pittsburgh bride who favors slim suits and fashionable frocks. When she was getting married, all of the pages she ripped out of bridal magazines and that she brought with her when she went dress shopping featured sheath dresses and simple designs à la the wedding dress of the late Caroline Bessette Kennedy. At each bridal shop she visited, this was the look she asked for and

Dressing for Success

Here are some wedding-dress silhouettes that look good on various body types.

- *Fuller figure:* Go for an A-line silhouette, which flatters most bodies. Avoid body-hugging looks as well as frills or flounces, which may make you look heavier. To create a slimmer shape, search out a dress with vertical lines (albeit subtle ones), such as in the beading on the bodice, which will work to elongate your look.

- *Petite stature:* Look for a dress with only a few details or a simple silhouette so the dress doesn't overwhelm you.

- *Small chest and shoulders:* You'll have many dress options because a small top can be very flattering in a wedding received. Despite the clarity of her fashion sense, however, Carla couldn't find the dress of her dreams. An astute salesperson at the last shop she visited suggested that Carla look at a different kind of dress, which might flatter her body in a way she never envisioned. Because Carla hadn't found the right dress yet, she agreed to try on the dress. What the salesperson presented was a Victorian-looking gown with tiny buttons up the back, a corseted bodice and delicate ruffles around the three-quarter-length sleeves—basically, a look that was completely opposite of what Carla had anticipated liking.

gown. If you'd like to make your bust look bigger, however, you can go with a bodice that features texture and detail, such as lace or beading, or you can wear "uplifting" under-garments, such as a padded or push-up bra.

- *Large bust:* Try to stay away from plunging necklines, unless you want to show cleavage, as well as intricately detailed bodices. Also, dresses with bolero jackets are not a good bet, because they don't fit smoothly over larger chests. A flattering look for this type of body is a dress with a halter-top design or, for those who would like to cover up their upper arms, three-quarter-length sleeves. For truly ample busts, steer clear of strapless gowns: you'll probably spend the whole affair pulling up on your dress for fear that you're going to fall out of it.

Once Carla tried this dress on, she knew she'd found the right dress for her. Although all the sheath dresses had been pretty on her fit figure, this completely different dress played up the curves she had and flattered her petite bustline. In addition, its ecru hue looked fabulous with Carla's olive skin and dark hair.

Bring Along Reinforcements — But Just a Few

One of the other reasons that Carla's dress-buying experience wasn't too exhausting, despite her trying on multiple dresses before finding the one she wanted, was because she went shopping with one girlfriend only — not her entire family. "If you have too many opinions to consider, you're really going to end up confused," says Forden. So, because you can't bring your fiancé with you to buy your dress, ask one or maybe two people whose opinions and taste you trust to go shopping with you. Avoid those who you think may have a preconceived notion of how a bride should dress — for instance, that the bride should cover her shoulders when you love the strapless look. And remember this: the old saying that too many cooks can spoil the stew is especially true when it comes to wedding dress shopping — or any other wedding planning, for that matter. So, KISS — keep it (your support system) simple, sweetheart.

Wedding Wisdom

My wedding dress is A-line and strapless. An A-line hides a lot and is very flattering.

MELISSA, IOWA

A HEALTHY WEIGHT FOR YOU

Despite spending the first half of this chapter asking that you learn to love your body, I do realize that there are times when a prewedding weight-loss plan makes sense — especially if you've been meaning to take off a few pounds and an upcoming wedding is just the incentive you need. I say, "Go for it!" if you've discussed your proposed weight-loss plan with your physician and he or she has given you a thumbs-up. Finally, I say, "Awesome!" if you're planning on losing weight in a slow and steady fashion, and you're developing eating and exercise habits that will last a lifetime (as discussed in Chapter 1), not just to get you to your wedding day wearing a size six.

> **Wedding Wisdom**
> *I ended up choosing a strapless gown—the last style I ever would have thought because I wanted to de-emphasize my bust. However, I found one with an asymmetrical bodice— the material was swept to one side—and it really looked perfect.*
> SARA, NEW YORK

Now that you're ready to start, the first thing to do is get a reasonable assessment of what you should weigh based on your height and age. A great way to do that is to make an appointment with a registered dietitian (log onto the American Dietetics Association at eatright.org to find an R.D. near you) or join a sensible weight-loss program like Weight Watchers. These professionals can help you target a weight that makes the most sense for you, and you may just find that the weight they're targeting is pounds beyond what you expected—meaning you have less to lose than you thought.

"With many of the brides-to-be who come to see me, I start by asking them what their desired body weight is, and they come up with this number," says Dominique Adair, M.S., R.D., a nutrition programs coordinator for New York Sports Club in New York City. "I ask them to subtract twelve pounds from that desired number. Next, I ask them to add twelve pounds to that desired number. We talk a little bit about what it would take to reach each weight, and then I ask them, 'If you had your choice, which would you rather be—twelve pounds over or twelve pounds under your desired body weight?'" Adair says that most women answer that they'd like to be underweight, which is amazing yet understandable because most of the svelte models and actresses featured on television, in advertisements, and on fashion pages are underweight. However, being underweight can be as unhealthy as being grossly overweight. "I find that this exercise is a great way to open a dialogue about the certain standards women set based on a number on the scale, rather than the fact that the weight twelve pounds over their desired weight is actually more healthy for them to be and probably is easier for them to attain and maintain," she adds.

"Many women have a false perception of what they should weigh," Adair continues. "Sometimes it's based on their history, such as 'I weighed 110 pounds when I graduated college.' But then I need to find out if they were eating healthfully at that weight or overexercising, and that gets us talking about whether 110 is really a reasonable weight for them to weigh now—or if it ever was."

Another issue that Adair brings up with clients as they grapple for an ideal weight is to what lengths these women are willing to go to get to a certain weight—and why. "If you dieted like crazy for the next six months, you wouldn't have the energy you need to plan your wedding, and you might get sick," she says. "Plus, why is it that people measure the success of their wedding on whether they get to a certain weight?"

There is a lot of talk in the dietary community about "set point value" and whether it is a reality or a myth. *Set point value* is supposedly the weight at which your body is most comfortable—and

> **Wedding Wisdom**
>
> *Having lost twenty pounds made me feel more self-confident at all of the prewedding events as well as at the wedding festivities. I was able to wear all the clothes that I wanted. Plus, it just made me feel so good inside that I conquered the one goal I had set for myself such a long time ago—losing weight.*
>
> AMY, TEXAS

you're most comfortable maintaining. Adair believes it is a weight that many women have achieved at one point in their lives when they weren't actively dieting or overexercising. They were eating healthfully, getting exercise on a regular basis, and probably didn't need to worry too much about what the scale said.

Can you think back to a time when this described your lifestyle? Perhaps it's how you're living now and therefore you really shouldn't stress yourself out about losing additional weight for your wedding. But if this lifestyle was five or more pounds ago, then by all means you can try to achieve it again before your wedding—just make sure to talk to a professional first. I don't advocate trying to accomplish any weight loss via fad-diet tactics. You'll just end up hungry, sick, and tired, which is hardly the state of mind for a balanced bride.

Once you and your doctor, registered dietitian, or Weight Watchers leader (or similar kind of professional) have decided on the right weight for you, please be realistic about your expectations. The average person loses between one-half pound and one pound per week when they eat appropriately and work out regularly, but weight loss is in no way a linear occurrence. Although you may think that with fifty-two weeks to go until your wedding, a twenty-five-pound weight loss is a no-brainer, think again.

"You won't keep losing a half pound each week as you go," warns Adair. "Your weight may drop more, stay the same, or go up." If you look at a weight-loss curve on a chart, it will eventually go down over time, but there will be lots of peaks and valleys in between. That's why you've got to be reasonable about how much weight you can— or should try to—lose before your wedding.

I say that you should scale back your expectations not only so that you avoid disappointment, but also because continuing to lose weight as your wedding day approaches could cause some serious problems in your plans, such as with your wedding dress. Recently, Ann, a bride-to-be, and her fiancé joined a gym and started seeing a registered dietitian. Both had wanted to lose weight, and a new life together was the perfect inspiration for adopting a healthier lifestyle—and more fit bodies. At their first meeting with the registered dietitian, about nine months before their wedding, they determined that Ann's goal weight was about thirty pounds less than what Ann weighed that day—and about ten pounds more than what Ann thought she should weigh! With this new and reasonable number in her head, plus a new understanding of how to eat a healthy low-fat diet and exercise regularly, Ann's weight-loss task seemed very doable.

By the time Ann started going dress shopping, she was twelve pounds lighter and feeling fabulous. At the first dress shop she visited, she found the gown she loved. Then she discovered something that was potentially troubling: in about six to eight weeks, she would have to return to the shop for a final dress fitting. This date was still weeks before her wedding and pounds away from her goal. Ann didn't know what to do when she E-mailed me for advice: should she stop losing weight now or should she continue losing up until her wedding day and hope that her dress would look fine? I suggested she do something in between and that was this: figure out exactly when she would have to go for her final fitting, and get used to the idea that whatever she weighed on that day should be the weight goal she should try to maintain through her wedding date. If that weight was still higher than the goal she'd originally set, then she could continue on her weight-loss path *after* the wedding. But now that she would have a wedding gown being made to fit her body based on that last fitting, it wouldn't be a good idea to continue losing weight, thus causing more stress and additional dress fittings down the line. Ann discussed this situation with her registered dietitian, who agreed with my advice and helped Ann craft a maintenance plan so that she wouldn't drop any significant weight after her final dress fitting.

Ann ended up taking off five additional pounds before the big day, even though she was trying to maintain her weight, and lucky for her, the dress still looked terrific on her. Because she had continued to eat well and exercise throughout, she was radiant as well. Now back from the honeymoon, Ann has restarted her weight-loss plan and is well on her way to reaching her goal.

IDEAS ON EXERCISE

Most adults understand intellectually what it takes to lose weight: you eat less and move more. In reality, however, very few people actually follow this combination, and then they wonder why their pants are getting tighter or their stomach seems flabbier than ever. While Chapter 1 offers the nuts and bolts of good nutrition, this section of Chapter 2 tackles the exercise portion of the weight-loss equation. (Note: please speak with your doctor before starting to exercise. You need to make sure your increase in activity won't put you at any risk for adverse health effects.)

To have a more fit body, you've got to use it in a way that raises your heart rate. In addition, you need to tax and stretch your muscles, because strength training and stretching are as important a component of exercise as cardiovascular work is. Most importantly, when it comes to exercise, you've got to be doing something you enjoy, that works well with your lifestyle, and that helps you reach your fitness goals. For one person, that might mean a gym membership. For another, it could be at-home fitness videos. For me, it's walking—something I can do outside in my neighborhood when the weather is nice or inside on my treadmill when it's raining, snowing, or too cold to venture out.

If you're having trouble figuring out the best fitness plan for you, all hope isn't lost. "You may think you hate exercise because you never liked aerobics," says Joan Price, fitness professional and author of *Joan Price Says, Yes, You Can Get in Shape* (Pacifica Press, 1996) and coauthor of *Complete Idiot's Guide to Online Health and Fitness* (Macmillan, 1999). But maybe you just never liked aerobics. Therefore, joining a health club to take a step aerobics class is probably not a good option for you, because you'll never enjoy it. Here's a way to find a fitness plan you'll surely follow.

"Think back to your childhood and teen years, when activities were fun and weren't qualified as exercise," Price suggests. "What did you love to do?" If your answer was ice-skating or roller-skating with friends, then maybe you need to visit an ice-skating rink on a regular basis or invest in a pair of in-line skates as your way of getting physical activity. If you were a basketball or soccer player, perhaps you should find an adult league to join, where you'll have fun and get your exercise as well. Finally, maybe you loved to dance, so taking up ballet is the best bet. Or, if you'd like to kill two birds with one stone, maybe you and your fiancé should sign up for swing or ballroom dancing lessons so you can learn a skill you'll use at your wedding reception—and for the rest of your life, for that matter—and get a workout to boot. In classes like this, says Price, "you may end up accumulating two or three hours' worth of dancing by the end of the evening."

Regardless of the activity you choose, you're going to have to be active three to five days a week to reap the full benefits. So, if you're going to select dance lessons once or twice a week as your fitness fun, you'll need to supplement your activity with something else. But here's the good news: you can get the rest of your activity in little bites throughout the week. "Ten minutes of exercise here and there has almost the same effect for health and weight-loss reasons as doing all of your exercise at once," says Price. "It just doesn't condition your heart as well as sustained exercise."

Everyday Exercise

There are many other creative ways to get physical activity into your everyday routine. One of my favorites is only going food shopping when I'm low on everything. That way I know I'll walk the whole store, and I'll be pushing a heavy cart at the same time. (Did you know that a trip to the average suburban-size grocery store during which you go up and down every aisle lets you cover about a quarter mile—more in a supercenter?) In addition, I leave shopping in the perimeter of the store for last so that I have to walk the full width of the supermarket at least once as I finish stocking my shopping cart. Here are some other tips for sneaking in exercise:

• *Avoid elevators and take the stairs.* Whether you live or work in a high-rise or are simply shopping at the mall, don't take the easy way up by riding the elevator or escalator. Instead, whenever you can, walk the stairs. It's a great way to condition your body and your heart.

• *Walk to places nearby.* If you need to do a slew of errands during your lunch hour, consider doing one of the following: leave the car at the office and walk to all of your errands. Or park your car at the last store you'll visit, and walk to all of the places where you need to go, ending up at the store nearest to your car.

• *Exit early from buses, trains, and automobiles.* If you take public transportation to work, get off a few stops early from the bus, train, or trolley, and walk to your office. When I lived in New York City, on my way to work I would exit the subway on the first midtown stop on my train line, which was still about twenty blocks from my office. On the way home, I would walk the twenty blocks back to that subway station and catch the train home. It was the perfect way to work in two twenty-minute walks, five days a week.

• *Do weight lifting with household items.* As you're carrying the jugs of milk in from grocery shopping, do some arms curls with them. You can do the same with bags of groceries. Additionally, instead of placing your laundry basket on a table when folding, put it on the floor and

Fitting in Fitness

Fitness expert Joan Price offers three additional ways to ensure that fitness is a doable part of your day. First, she suggests keeping a fitness log. That is, make an appointment with yourself each day to get exercise. Write it down in your daily calendar or enter it in your digital organizer. Second, create a physical reminder to do your exercise. That could include always having your workout gear in the car or arranging to walk with a neighbor in the morning. With the latter, you've got someone else counting on you, which is a good incentive not to blow off exercise. And third, tell yourself that you'll only do five minutes' worth of exercise and then you have permission to come home. Chances are, once those five minutes come and go, you'll already be feeling good and want to continue with your full workout. But on the days when you're not feeling well or when the weather is not cooperating, you can stop and say, "That's enough for today."

squat each time you reach for an article of clothing. You'll end up doing a fitness class worth of squats with each load of laundry you fold.

• *Stretch it out.* A good fitness plan comprises three parts: aerobic activity, strength training, and stretching. Most people skimp on the stretching because they don't think it's important, but being flexible and stretching regularly as part of your exercise routine is the key to avoiding injury. I found this out firsthand recently when my doctor pointed out that my once pliable but now-taut hamstrings were the culprit behind my chronically sore back. Once I started stretching, the pain went away. I suggest you attend a yoga class or arrange for a few meetings with a personal trainer to pick up good stretching techniques.

BALANCE: THE BOTTOM LINE

I implore all brides to understand that loving yourself for who you are goes a lot further than numbers on a scale or a dress size in clothing. That's why, unless there is a health or medical reason for you to lose weight—and your doctor gives you the green light to do so—don't fall into the prewedding weight-loss trap like I did and try to drop unnecessary pounds before the big day. Remember, your fiancé loves you for who you are now, not a weight you think you should weigh.

In addition, loving yourself for who you are will help you achieve an inner calm when it comes time to buy a wedding dress. Instead of trying to fit into a dress that you once saw a model in a magazine wear, go for a gown that plays up your assets while playing down your liabilities. That's the kind of dress that will make you feel like a truly beautiful bride.

Finally, a great way to learn to love your body is to start using it in a physical activity that you enjoy—whether it is ice-skating or surfing. Not only will a regular exercise routine help you develop stronger muscles and bones, it will also help decrease your stress and possibly improve your relationship with your future husband. Says fitness expert Joan Price, "You can walk, dance, or skate your stress off instead of taking it into your relationship."

3

PREWEDDING HEALTH CHECKUP

IN THE NEXT chapter I talk about the importance of planning before your wedding what kind of birth control method you'll use in married life—that is, unless you're planning to start a family right away. But in this chapter, I want to talk a little bit about your overall health, including your dental health, and why you should keep preventative practices at the top of your mind. This isn't so much to prevent you from falling ill on your wedding day, although I've heard of plenty of brides and grooms who were fighting fever and hallucinations during a full-fledged bout of the flu as they walked down the aisle. (Note to winter brides and grooms: make sure you add getting a flu shot to your to-do list!) Rather, to be a balanced bride—and groom, for that matter—it would be ideal if you could start your life together with your health in tip-top shape. Not only will having a thorough checkup give you a better idea of how healthy your body is, but it will also tell you where you need to do a little bit more preventative work. In addition, when you finally decide to start a family, you'll already be on the path to good health.

Good health is more than just about feeling good. According to Michael P. Zimring, M.D., a general internist at Mercy Medical Center in Baltimore, Maryland, sometimes the real value in a checkup comes more from discussing a person's family history than the exams themselves. "If I have a patient in his twenties who tells me that his father had a heart attack and died when he was forty-five," Dr. Zimring says, "I'm going to make sure I check his cholesterol and monitor it over the long term so this guy doesn't drop dead at a young age." (Higher-than-average cholesterol is often linked to a greater risk of heart disease, including heart attacks.) Likewise, if Dr. Zimring has a female patient who reveals that her mother and grandmother both died from ovarian cancer, he's going to make sure that a key component of her overall care includes a regular and thorough gynecological exam. That way if any symptoms of ovarian cancer crop up, he can catch them early. "Someone who has had two first-line relatives get ovarian cancer has a 50 percent chance of getting ovarian cancer," he says, "so you want to know about these things ahead of time."

CHECKUP CHECKLIST

Even though discussing family history is a big component of preventative health care, certain exams do have their place in your medical care. To give you a sense of what kinds of tests you and your fiancé can expect to get when seeing your doctor for this or any other checkup in the future, I've put together the following list of suggested regular medical exams for both women and men, based on age. (Note: if you have a family history of certain kinds of diseases, your doctor may suggest that you have certain exams done earlier than your peers, say, a mammogram in your twenties if women in your family have had breast cancer at a young age.) Mine is just a suggested timeline for these exams and should not be used to replace advice, care, or suggestions from your doctor. In addition, I'm not presenting this information in any order of importance. In other words, they aren't ranked. That means that you should not exclude one exam at the expense of the others simply because of where it falls on the list. All of these tests are important and should be routinely done. If you have questions about any of these tests, please see your doctor. Finally, women's tests are arranged in different age categories than men's simply because there are many specific exams that women need during their twenties, thirties, and forties, whereas the age of fifty is the cutoff for men's exams.

Women Up to Age Thirty-Five

□ Have your blood pressure checked every time you see a doctor or at least annually.
□ See your dentist twice a year.
□ Once a month, do a breast self-exam.
□ Have an annual Pap smear and pelvic exam.
□ Get a full physical every five years.
□ Once every two years, have a full cholesterol screening done.
□ Ask your primary-care physician for a referral to a dermatologist so you can have a full-body check for unusual moles or skin growths, which might signal a kind of skin or other cancer.

> **Wedding Wisdom**
> *This was the year for physicals for us, and we went full force about six months before the wedding. We also took care of our teeth at the dentist. It's a good idea to get checked out before you get married so you don't get hit with any unexpected medical news.*
> MARGARET, TEXAS

Women Ages Thirty-Five to Fifty

□ Have your blood pressure checked every time you see a doctor or at least annually.

☐ Through age forty, get a complete checkup every three years; after age forty, your doctor may ask you to come in for a checkup every year or every other year.

☐ At age forty, expect to start going annually or biannually for mammograms. However, some doctors may order a baseline mammogram at age thirty-five or younger.

☐ See your dentist twice a year.

☐ Have an annual Pap smear, pelvic exam, and breast exam done at the doctor's office.

☐ Once a month, do a breast self-exam.

☐ Ask your primary-care physician for a referral to a dermatologist so you can have a full-body check for unusual moles or skin growths, which might signal a kind of skin or other cancer.

☐ Between ages thirty-five and forty, get your cholesterol checked every two years; up that frequency to once a year after age forty.

Women Age Fifty and Above

☐ Have your blood pressure checked every time you see a doctor or at least annually.

☐ Schedule a complete checkup each year.

☐ See your dentist twice a year.

☐ Once a month, do a breast self-exam.

☐ Have an annual Pap smear, pelvic exam, and breast exam done at the doctor's office.

☐ Ask your primary-care physician for a referral to a dermatologist so you can have a full-body check for unusual moles or skin growths, which might signal a kind of skin or other cancer.

☐ Focus on the health of your colon: have an annual digital rectal exam and a fecal occult blood test (basically, checking a stool sample for the presence of blood).

- Every five years, get a flexible sigmoidoscopy exam, which is part of the screening for colorectal cancer.
- Every ten years, have a colonoscopy, which is part of the screening for colorectal cancer.

Men Up to Age Fifty

- Have your blood pressure checked every time you see a doctor or at least annually.
- From ages thirty to thirty-nine, have a full physical checkup with your internist or primary-care physician every three years. From ages forty to forty-nine, have a physical every two years. Once you hit fifty, have an annual physical exam.
- See your dentist twice a year.
- Once a month, perform a testicular self-exam.
- Ask your primary-care physician for a referral to a dermatologist so you can have a full-body check for unusual moles or skin growths, which might signal a kind of skin or other cancer.
- Once every five years, have a full cholesterol screening done.

Men Age Fifty and Above

- Have your blood pressure checked every time you see a doctor or at least annually.
- Start going for annual physical checkups.
- Get an annual screening for prostate cancer.
- Focus on the health of your colon: have an annual digital rectal exam and a fecal occult blood test (basically, checking a stool sample for the presence of blood).
- Every five years, get a flexible sigmoidoscopy, which is part of the screening for colorectal cancer.
- Every ten years, have a colonoscopy, which is part of the screening for colorectal cancer.

- ☐ See your dentist twice a year.
- ☐ Ask your primary-care physician for a referral to a dermatologist so you can have a full-body check for unusual moles or skin growths, which might signal a kind of skin or other cancer.
- ☐ Once every five years, have a full cholesterol screening done.

DOING SELF-EXAMS

You'll notice that in my checkup checklist I list two kinds of self-exams that should be done monthly—a breast self-exam for women and a testicular self-exam for men. Both are excellent ways of detecting cancer early, but perhaps not for the reason you think.

Self-exams are so important because they allow you and your fiancé to become better acquainted with how your body feels and looks (your breasts, his testicles) normally. That means if there is a slight deviation from what feels or looks normal—a new lump in the breast or testicle, slight puckering in your breast tissue, or discharge from your nipple—you'll notice it right away. You should immediately discuss any changes with your doctor.

If you or your fiancé are not comfortable touching your own bodies or looking at yourselves naked in the mirror, please get over this issue right away. Otherwise, you may not be able to do a self-exam properly. Every self-exam is comprised of two parts—palpating the breasts or testicles *and* looking at yourselves in the mirror naked.

Breast Self-Exam

Because a woman's breasts tend to be tender, engorged, and lumpy when she's premenstrual, the American Cancer Society recommends that a woman do a breast self-exam about a week after her period ends. That way you won't mistake the lumpy state of your breast, which is normal before your period, or any tenderness (also normal) for a problem. (If you're not menstruating, pick a date on the calendar, such as the first of the month, and plan to do your exam on that day every month. Women with breast implants or who've previously had a mastectomy need to do monthly self-exams as well.)

You can perform your exam lying down or standing in the shower, although doing both is the most thorough method. Since you can feel deeper in your breast if your fingers slide easily over your skin, use lotion or, in the shower, soap on your breast.

To manually examine your breasts, start by raising one hand over your head. Then, using the fingers of your opposite hand, gently but firmly palpate your breast in small circles (think about drumming your fingers on a desk to get the correct effect) as you move around your breast. Cover the entire breast in this circular motion. Then, using the same drumming motion, palpate from the outer breast toward the nipple area, again covering the entire breast as you go. Be sure to also check along your collarbone as well as the tissue from your outer breast to your underarm. Do the same on the other breast.

For the visual part of the self-exam, stand topless in front of a mirror. Raise your arms over your head and then put your hands on your hips, all the while looking at your breasts for any changes in shape, such as puckering or swelling. Should you see or feel anything different, no matter how remote, call your doctor right away for an appointment.

For a visual reminder that you can keep in the shower with you, order the waterproof "Breast Self-Exam Card" from the Susan G. Komen Breast Cancer Foundation, which includes instructions on the proper way to do a breast self-exam. Go to the foundation's website at breastcancerinfo.com, enter your mailing address, and they'll send you one for free.

Testicular Self-Exam

A testicular self-exam should be a two-handed event—that is, your fiancé should use both of his hands to examine each of his testicles. The correct way to examine the testicle is to gently roll the testicle between the fingers of each hand, feeling for any lumps or abnormal swelling. This exam shouldn't hurt your fiancé; if he experiences pain, he should talk to his doctor about this discomfort. Tell him not to worry if one testicle feels larger than the other. Just like some women have one larger breast, men have the same with their testicles. Finally, testicles are a lumpy lot, so as long as a lump doesn't change in shape, size, or location from month to month, it shouldn't be a cause for concern. However, if he is worried about anything seemingly abnormal in his testicles or scrotal area, have him see his doctor.

In addition to feeling the testicles, your fiancé should examine the epididymis, which is behind the testicles. It may feel lumpy and suspicious the first couple of times he examines it, but not to worry: the epididymis is normally quite textured.

Your fiancé should also give his scrotum a visual once-over on a monthly basis, looking for any changes in size or shape. Again, encourage him to report anything out of the ordinary to his doctor.

Finally, you and your fiancé should be aware that some symptoms of testicular cancer do not involve the testicles at all, including a dull ache in the abdomen or groin as well as tenderness and enlargement of his breast area. If he experiences any of these, make an appointment right away with his physician.

DENTAL DETAILS

I'm sure you know that seeing your dentist every six months is part of a good care routine, but if you're anything like me, you put off seeing the dentist because of deep-seated fears. But every time I go, I feel great, my smile looks awesome, and I never experience any pain. So why am I hesitant to go? I really can't tell you.

What I *can* tell you is this: gone are the days when dentists told their patients to "grin and bear it" and that pain relief medications like Novocain were unnecessary for filling cavities or, worse, getting a root canal. "Long after the physical pain goes away, the emotional scars remain," says Jerry Gordon, D.M.D., a dentist in private practice in Bensalem, Pennsylvania. Besides the fear of pain, Dr. Gordon believes many patients are afraid of being scolded for not brushing their teeth or not seeing the dentist often enough. But dentists aren't there to yell at you: they're there to help you take care of your teeth. My childhood dentist had a sign in his office, which I still remember to this day. It read, "If you ignore your teeth, they'll go away." How true it is. If you don't take care of your teeth and disease sets in, your teeth will go away because they'll fall out. And let's be honest: the gap-toothed look is cute on young children only.

But extreme scenarios aside, here are two reasons to visit your dentist before your wedding. One, if you don't take care of any cavities or tooth pain beforehand, you could end up with an abscessed tooth or an oral

> **Wedding Wisdom**
> *Despite years of orthodontics, I still have a crooked smile and would have to get braces again to fix it. With little time or budget, this was pretty much out of the question, but I did make sure to go to my dentist for regular cleanings. I also splurged and got my teeth whitened, which did make a nice difference for all the photographs. It was definitely worth it.*
> CHANA, MASSACHUSETTS

infection on your honeymoon. That will surely put a damper on the romance. And two, if you are self-conscious about your smile and would like to improve it in time for your wedding pictures, your dentist can help you do that.

Dental Dos and Don'ts

Want further proof that taking care of your pearly whites is good medicine? If you don't floss and brush regularly, you can end up with all kinds of oral infections, which lead to bad breath. Now, who wants to knock 'em dead with her breath on her wedding day? Here are other dental dos and don'ts to keep in mind:

- *Don't stop brushing and flossing if your gums bleed.* "People think it's their toothbrush that's causing the bleeding, so they cut back on their brushing," says Dr. Jerry Gordon, a dentist in Bensalem, Pennsylvania. Actually, bleeding is a sign of gum disease, or gingivitis. Left untreated, it could lead to bone loss and then tooth loss. So despite their instincts, the worst thing people with bleeding gums can do is stop brushing and flossing. In fact, they should do the opposite—step up both—and call their dentist as soon as possible to schedule an appointment.

- *Don't assume oral pain is normal.* Although the occasional twinge when eating ice cream may be normal, pain in general or regularly when eating is a sign that something's

I only wish tooth whitening was an affordable option for when I got married. You see, because of frequent antibiotics use and high fevers as a child, my adult teeth have always been slightly discolored. Although I generally like the way I look in pictures, I've always been

wrong. "The solution could be as simple as switching to a sensitive-tooth toothpaste or as complicated as having to fill multiple cavities," says Dr. Gordon. Bottom line: leave the evaluation as to the cause of pain up to your dentist. Don't attempt to do it yourself, and don't ignore your discomfort, especially if it's persistent and affects your quality of life—for example, you've had to give up hot coffee and soup because drinking or eating them hurts too much.

- *Don't think you can put off seeing the dentist.* "One of the reasons dentists like to see patients every six months is that so often dental problems are insidious, or without symptoms, so they sneak up on you," says Dr. Gordon. "But if you're getting in my chair every six months, chances are I'll be able to spot that problem when it's still small and easy and inexpensive to fix." For example, filling a few cavities will set you back about $100 each, assuming insurance won't cover it. Let those cavities go without treatment, however, and the infection will grow. Then, instead of just a cavity, you may be looking at a root canal, which may also require a crown, and suddenly your dental bill is adding up to a whopping $1,000 or more.

aware that my teeth were a little more yellow than I'd prefer. So last summer, many years after I'd been married but wanting to do something nice for myself, I spent three hours and about $375 (prices vary according to dentists) in my dentist's office having my teeth whitened. First, the dentist smeared a special gel on my teeth and then zapped them with a laser. After the procedure was done, he sent me home with supplies that I could use on a regular basis for touch-up whitening. They included tooth trays and whitening gel. Every few months since the initial procedure, I fill each tray with a little bit of gel, pop them on my teeth, and a few hours later (or the next morning, if I wear them while I sleep), my teeth are brighter and whiter.

Besides tooth whitening (which can be done in an office, like I had done, or using tooth trays exclusively and at home), Dr. Gordon says a number of cosmetic dentistry options are available to help improve your smile by the time you get married:

Wedding Wisdom

Because I was going to be moving across the country after the wedding, I did not know how long it would be before I got set up with new doctors in my new hometown. So I saw my dentist one last time and got my teeth cleaned. I even saw my dermatologist and asked him for any tips on keeping my skin looking great until the wedding.

SHARAYU, OREGON

• *Tooth shaping.* In this pain-free procedure, the dentist uses an instrument to shape teeth so that they're more aesthetically pleasing. This may involve shortening canines or rounding teeth that look too square or too long.

• *Filling replacements.* Many adults have mouths full of metal—fillings, that is. If any of your front teeth have them, you know how they can take on a grayish appearance over time. Dr. Gordon suggests replacing metal fillings with white or clear ones.

• *Bonding*. During this process, the dentist takes a white composite resin and dabs it on parts of or an entire tooth to enhance its appearance.

• *Porcelain veneers*. "This is the Mercedes of treatments," says Dr. Gordon. Prices start at about $4,000. Think of this cosmetic treatment as similar to putting on false fingernails: the dentist will create custom-made veneers and bond them to the front of your teeth.

• *Braces*. More orthodontics than cosmetic dentistry, this is a good option if your teeth are misaligned and the other cosmetic procedures mentioned here won't fix the problem. Good news for adults considering braces: there is a new clear-plastic kind of braces on the market that are nearly invisible.

> **Wedding Wisdom**
> *I wanted my teeth to be nearly perfect for the wedding, so a year beforehand I had my top and then my bottom teeth bleached. After I achieved the color I wanted, I had porcelain veneers put on two of my front teeth that needed work. The photos turned out great.*
> KAREN, MARYLAND

For more information on cosmetic dentistry, see Dr. Gordon's website at dentalcomfortzone.com.

BALANCE: THE BOTTOM LINE

Doctors don't call it preventive medicine for nothing—regular checkups at the doctor and dentist help *prevent* many, many illnesses. That's why a prewedding health checkup as well as seeing your doctor on a regular basis—and following the prescription of my checkup checklist, including monthly self-exams—makes for good medicine. You want to be as healthy as you can be for your big day and beyond.

Now is also the time to take care of your mouth, especially if you have any painful teeth or a bite that makes you want to frown, not smile. Remember: you're going to be the focus of a lot of pictures on your wedding day, so why not make your smile the brightest it can be? Also, putting oral care at the top of your medical to-do list will help ensure that painful cavities or an oral infection won't ruin your honeymoon.

Wedding Wisdom

I got braces on my teeth before my wedding so I'd have a perfectly straight smile.

LESLIE, NEW YORK

4

FAMILY PLANNING

WE'VE ALL HEARD of the crass wedding guest who, in the middle of the reception, starts quizzing the bride and groom on when they're going to start a family. This tactic seems totally tacky—and it is. When a couple decides to have children is a private matter, and surely hours after they've walked down the aisle is not when they'll be in the mood to discuss their family plans for the future. But despite how inappropriate this topic seems on your wedding day, it's actually something that you'd better discuss before you get married—not after—because the decision to have children (or not) must be mutually agreed-upon for a marriage to work.

Let me put it another way: if you want children and your fiancé doesn't, or vice versa, you cannot get married thinking, "Oh, he'll change his mind once we're married and he sees how wonderful life is as husband and wife. He is sure to want to have children then." Sure, sometimes people *do* change their minds on certain issues—sometimes even when it involves having children—but you can't go into your marriage assuming this will happen. If one of you doesn't want to have kids, you've got to prepare yourself for the worst-case scenario where future children are concerned—that there won't be any. So, if you and your fiancé are at an impasse over having children, yet you're committed to getting married, then you really need to seek professional guidance. As I say time and time again in this book, communication and compromise are the cornerstones of a solid, happy marriage, and you'll need to use both as you work through how, when, or even if children will be a part of your future family. Because having children is a given in most marriages, if you and your fiancé don't share a view on children in your future, it's imperative that you speak to a counselor right away. Covering this territory won't be easy, but you have to do it and do it now.

BABIES R US?

There are many reasons that someone may not want to have kids. All are valid and need to be discussed. Keep in mind that the desire to have children is often as strong as the desire not to have them. Furthermore, a person's ability to change the pro-children person's mind into not wanting to have kids is about as likely as making the anti-child person sign up for parenting classes. But, in rare instances and with plenty of communication, it can happen.

For example, when Bill and I first got together, I was pretty sure that I did not want to have children. I was not comfortable around children, probably the product of my being an only child, and I was so afraid of ending up like my parents—divorced—that I didn't want to subject any future children to such a possibility. In addition, while I was still dating, married couples I knew started having children, and I saw how hard they worked at taking care of their kids. It seemed like such a huge task that I wanted nothing to do with it.

Around the same time that Bill and I were becoming more serious with one another and began discussing our future together, I happened to be seeing a therapist. This gave me the opportunity to talk about my parenting misgivings with a professional, and here's what that professional helped me discover: the primary reason I was opposed to having children was because, in my mind, mothers parented alone, as I saw my mother doing. Obviously, mine was a very skewed view of the parenting world, based on my own family dynamic of being an only child of divorced parents. As I became aware of my prejudice and could talk about it, not only with my therapist but with Bill as well, I realized that my relationship with Bill did not have to follow the same path of my parents. In fact, with Bill as my partner, I began to feel confident that we would be just that—partners—in our marriage and, should we have children, in our role as parents. I'm happy to report that we now have two beautiful daughters, and I can't imagine what my life would be like if I weren't a mother. Of course, I felt nervous, scared, and uncomfortable when my children were first born—I mean, what did I know about taking care of a child? But I soon realized that *all* new parents share this trepidation.

I realize that I've just presented a scenario where all the loose ends got tied up into a nice, neat package, and the couple lived happily ever after with kids. That's not to say that if you or your fiancé are unsure about whether you want to have kids that you can go about changing the other person's mind. But what my experience shows is how valuable getting professional counseling can be for your relationship. I can say now with confidence that had I not sought a therapist's help, I don't think I would have ended up marrying Bill, let alone giving birth to our children. Sure, I loved him, but we had very different views of the future—his with kids, mine without. Thanks to my therapist, I was able to envision a future with kids as well and to feel good about that future.

So, how can you two determine if and when children make the most sense for your future together? Beyond asking yourselves the most pressing question of "Do we want to have kids?" I suggest you also ask yourselves each of the following questions.

Can You Afford a Baby?

A recent *U.S News and World Report* article stated that, through college, the average middle-income family should expect to invest more than one million dollars in a child—from the cost of birth to paying for college. Obviously, that isn't chump change. That price tag is sure to rise if you find you can't get pregnant right away. Then you need to factor in treatments for infertility, which are not always covered by insurance and can set you back $50,000 or more. If having a baby on your own isn't in the cards and you choose to turn to adoption, expect to shell out a minimum of $15,000 in doing so. Add to this scenario the issue of one or both of you being in college or graduate school or thinking about going back to school, and you need to seriously consider whether your salary (or lack thereof) can support a growing family.

For my husband and me, though, time during his graduate school studies ended up being the ideal scenario for us to start a family. That's because we were lucky enough to have a unique set of circumstances come together that made those lean graduate school years not so lean and actually perfect for having children:

One, we moved from an expensive city to an affordable town—New York City to Ann Arbor, Michigan.

Two, my husband received a generous stipend from the University of Michigan, where he was getting his Ph.D., plus free health insurance for both of us. This insurance had no deductible, so all of my prenatal visits were free of charge. Our only out-of-pocket cost was upgrading to a private room in the hospital after the children were born. Total cost to us? Five dollars per child, or ten dollars total, to bring two healthy children into the world. (I kid you not.)

And three, at the time we moved to Michigan, I launched a writing business, which quickly became a lucrative venture. Plus, as a self-employed person, I could afford to continue working as much or as little as I wanted after my children were born, allowing us to avoid tight times.

Does Your Living Situation Make Sense for Children?

A couple who are still living with one of their parents, perhaps so they can save for a house, may find that this living situation is perfect for having children. That's because they can look to their parents as nearby and ready-made baby-sitters. Another couple living far away from family may want to wait until they can move closer to home—or their parents closer to them—so they have familial support during the first few years of their children's lives. Finally, you may live in an apartment or housing situation where you simply cannot fit another person. I've heard of many urban couples who converted a walk-in closet in their apartment to a baby's nursery, because they couldn't afford to move to a bigger space. Perhaps they should have planned their family around when they would be able to move to a roomier abode.

Can Your Careers Accommodate a Baby?

Is one of you willing to give up a career to raise children? For couples who work on the fast track, such as those vying for a partnership in a business, law firm, or medical practice, taking time off to have children may not be an option. This has nothing to do with maternity- or paternity-leave policies but rather your own timeline for reaching certain career goals over time. You may not be willing to put aside or put off these goals to start a family. If one of you isn't willing to stay home with the children—even for the short term—then you need to discuss how you feel about various day-care options. Maybe one of you is vehemently opposed to the idea of day care, and so you have to readdress the issue of who would be willing to put his or her career on hold while you start a family or, considering your views on day care, whether having children makes sense for you at all.

Are You Healthy Enough to Have Children?

"Someone with an alcohol or tobacco addiction will need to quit and go through withdrawal before becoming pregnant," says Juliana van Olphen Fehr, a certified nurse midwife and coordinator of the nurse midwifery education program at Shenandoah University in Winchester, Virginia. "That needs to be taken care of months, if not years, before you start a family." On the medical side, someone who is being treated for a disease would need to wait until he or she is given a clean bill of health before trying to conceive a child. Likewise, if one of you works in an environment where you are exposed to chemicals, toxins, or infectious diseases, or you're under severe amounts of stress all the time, you may be unknowingly risking your health and the health of your future children. If so, you may need to consider switching jobs for your health's sake before you get pregnant.

Furthermore, genetic counseling is a must if either of you has a family history of genetic disease, such as Tay-Sachs disease in Jewish families or sickle-cell anemia in African Americans. The counselor can help you determine your actual risk and help you figure out if having a baby of your own makes sense.

Are You the Right Age?

Age can affect your health as well. If you're an older couple considering having children, there is an increased risk of complications associated with pregnancy, although plenty of "older" woman have perfectly fine pregnancies. However, it is a reality that the older you are, the greater your risk for having a child with a genetic abnormality like Down's syndrome. According to the March of Dimes, a thirty-year-old woman has a one in 1,000 chance of having a baby with Down's syndrome. Only five years later, at age thirty-five, her risk more than doubles to one in 400, and by age forty, that chance has more than doubled again to one in 100. If you fall into this age category, then not only will you and your husband need to discuss if having a baby is right for you, but also if you would be able to handle a child with special needs. If you'll be over age thirty-five by the time you want to start a family, talk to a genetic counselor, who can present the pros and cons of pregnancy at your age.

Even after asking yourselves these questions, you still may not have an exact idea of when having a baby makes the most sense. That's OK. Maybe you could only come up with reasonable answers to two of these questions, but at least it got you talking. And like I've said before and will say many times again in this book, communication is one of the keys to a successful relationship, and that's what I want you to have—even if you still are uncertain about your future as a mother and father.

BIRTH CONTROL BASICS

Unless you're planning to start a family right away, you'll need to fig-ure out the best birth control method for you to use right now. This is especially critical if you're not waiting until you're married to have intercourse. There have been many brides who've had to have last-minute alterations of their wedding gowns to accommodate their expanding middles because they thought "it could never happen to me" and it did—they became pregnant before they got married—because they weren't careful about their use (or lack thereof) of birth control.

Although I don't mean to tread in the territory of seventh-grade health class, it's important to give you a refresher course in barrier methods, birth control pills, and other ways of preventing pregnancy—especially because there may be new options on the market that will fit better with your married lifestyle than they did when you were single and dating. I've broken the list into three categories: over-the-counter options, meaning those you can purchase at your local drugstore, pharmacy, or supermarket; prescription methods, which you'll need to see a doctor or other health-care provider to receive; and other options, including natural family planning. This last option may be your only choice if your religion or culture prohibits artificial means of birth control. Finally, this is just a sampling of the most common birth control methods. This list is in no way all-encompassing and should not be used as your only information source on birth control.

Before you indulge in any wedding-night intercourse or other sexual play—either before or after you're married—I urge you to meet with your health-care practitioner of choice and have a lengthy discussion on the pros and cons of every birth control method to help you decide which one works best for your lifestyle and your family-planning plan.

Over-the-Counter Choices

Condoms

A condom is a tubular-shaped sheath made of latex or another material that is placed on the penis and prevents sperm from entering the vagina. There is also a female condom, which is inserted into the vagina. Condoms made from latex are said to be the most reliable, especially when sexually transmitted diseases come into play. To prevent pregnancy, always make sure you put the condom on the penis or into the vagina before you have intercourse or any genital contact, and remove it immediately after ejaculation and before your partner's penis becomes flaccid. Otherwise, you risk semen leaking into the vagina. If you experience vaginal dryness, try a water-based lubricant (no petroleum jelly, thank you, because it will destroy the condom and negate its efficiency) to help things move along more comfortably and smoothly, so to speak.

PROS: Condoms are relatively inexpensive (about twelve dollars for a box of twenty-four), easy to use, and a good option for a woman who can't use hormonal contraception, for instance, because of a predisposition to migraine headaches. Also, if you decide to start your family and you're using condoms, you can do so right away because you needn't see a doctor to remove a device or wait a requisite period of time for a hormonal contraception to clear your body.

CONS: Success depends on using condoms properly, and some men may complain about a reduced sensation during intercourse. (One insensitive husband I know said that he'd gotten married so he could *stop* wearing condoms when he had sex!) If you used to use a non-barrier method of birth control, such as the Pill, but have decided to give condoms a go, you and your partner may not like having to interrupt lovemaking to put on the condom. Additionally, if you're interested in using the female condom, you may have trouble finding it, as some people have reported scant distribution of this newer birth control device.

RELIABILITY: Ranges from 90 percent to 98 percent. By coupling a condom with a spermicidal agent, such as a foam, you can increase the efficacy rate to 99.5 percent.

Spermicides

Spermicides come in a number of different forms—foam, cream, jelly, or suppository—but they all work the same way. You have to insert it into your vagina in advance of intercourse, where the spermicidal agent will act as a chemical barrier against sperm by immobilizing them.

PROS: Like condoms, a spermicide is easy to purchase and relatively easy to use.

CONS: There's no doubt about it, a spermicide is tough chemical stuff and therefore can be hard on sensitive skin, like the vaginal walls or the penis head. So, if you're easily irritated, this isn't a good birth control option for you. Also, because of the nature of the beast, spermicides are notoriously messy, thus increasing the "yuck" factor after sex.

Reliability: Not very good because there is no physical barrier against sperm, and the spermicidal agent isn't guaranteed to kill every sperm. Reliability rate has been shown to be as low as 74 percent.

Prescription Methods

Cervical Cap

This is a latex-covered dome about the size of a baby-bottle nipple that fits snugly over your cervix and acts as a barrier against sperm. In addition, prior to inserting, you fill the cap with spermicidal foam or jelly, like you would a diaphragm, and the spermicide acts as extra protection against sperm.

Pros: Can be left in place for up to forty-eight hours, meaning you don't have to hop up out of bed after intercourse to remove it right away and you can have sex multiple times while it is inserted, although Planned Parenthood recommends that you add spermicidal foam or jelly into the vagina via an applicator before having additional intercourse to be safe. A cap has a lifetime of about two years, so once you're fitted for it, you're set for twenty-four months. Because the shape of your cervix will change with childbirth, however, you can't go back to your old cap if you have had a baby in that two-year window. In fact, refitting after childbirth is a must, or you risk having two children very close in age.

Cons: Must be inserted before intercourse, which, like all barrier methods, can be a hassle. Also, according to Planned Parenthood, the cervical cap comes in only four sizes, so finding the perfect fit is negligible. Because a cervical cap is so small, proper insertion can be tough, and any variations on the perfect fit can make it less effective. Because it involves a visit to the doctor, getting a cervical cap can be pricey. Although your insurance may cover some or all of the cost, a cap runs about twenty-five dollars, plus the exam. Then you must buy spermicidal agents to put in the cap, which adds about ten dollars onto the price tag each time you replenish your supply.

RELIABILITY: As little as 80 percent or as great as 90 percent, depending on the circumstances.

Depo-Provera

Depo-Provera is a shot of progesterone, a hormone that inhibits ovulation, or the release of an egg. It is given in the arm or buttocks.

PROS: One shot of Depo-Provera helps to prevent pregnancy for three months.

CONS: Depo-Provera has been known to make women's periods heavier, and breakthrough bleeding during the month is commonplace. This bleeding can range from spotting on a daily basis to a light flow that doesn't follow a consistent pattern. Also, Depo-Provera may cause you to gain about five pounds in the first year you're on it and two to three pounds in subsequent years of use.

RELIABILITY: About 99.7 percent, mostly because there's no human factor to affect how well—or poorly—you use this method. However, please note that it is not 100 percent effective; only abstinence is.

Diaphragm

Like the cervical cap, the diaphragm is a latex dome that stops sperm from entering the cervix—and joining with an egg. A diaphragm must sit securely in the vagina and cover the cervix to work. Also like a cervical cap, it is filled with spermicide, which acts as an extra agent against sperm.

Pros: Costs about thirty dollars (although your insurance company may cover that cost), and it lasts for two years. Also, you can leave a diaphragm in place for up to twenty-four hours after intercourse, although you may want to remove it sooner—and empty your bladder right away—if you're prone to urinary tract infections. (Note: the diaphragm should remain in place for a minimum of six hours after the last act of intercourse because sperm stay alive in the vagina for many hours. If you remove it too soon, you increase your risk of getting pregnant.)

Cons: Diaphragms have been traced to urinary tract infections. That's because the diaphragm can put undue pressure on the urethra, the tube from the bladder. On another front, some doctors believe that weight gains and losses of more than ten pounds can affect a diaphragm's fit. So, if you're in the process of taking off weight, plan to be refitted for a new diaphragm with each ten pounds you lose, or choose an alternate birth control method until you reach your goal weight.

Reliability: Approximately 94 percent.

> *Wedding Wisdom*
>
> *We were sexually active from very early on, so we had discussed birth control nearly at the outset. I'd been using a diaphragm for years and that's what I continued to use, although we're talking about trying to start a family soon.*
>
> Kelly, Illinois

IUD

A doctor will insert this T-shaped device into the uterus to make the lining of the uterus unfavorable for pregnancy and to affect the motility of sperm. IUDs accomplish this task in two different ways. The copper IUD, marketed under the name Paragard, works when the copper in it reacts chemically with the lining of your uterus to make it hostile to sperm. The Mirena IUD, which was introduced in 2001, is a hormonal IUD. It contains levonorgestrel, a synthetic version of progesterone that it releases every day. What the progesterone does is thicken the cervical mucus, making it difficult for sperm to reach the uterus. It also thins the uterine lining so much that even if a sperm were to fertilize an egg, implantation in the uterus would be nearly impossible.

PROS: Once you have a copper IUD inserted, it is good for ten years. The Mirena IUD is good for five years. An IUD is a great birth control method for a woman who doesn't want to have children right away or doesn't want to think about her birth control method on a daily basis. Furthermore, because of Mirena's effect on the uterine lining, women's periods become lighter, possibly nonexistent, and it reduces cramping significantly. Finally, even though Mirena is a hormonal device, less than 3 percent of users complain of hormone-related side effects, such as headaches and breast tenderness. (Note: because cessation of menstruation has been linked with bone loss, talk with your health-care practitioner about taking calcium supplements in conjunction with this birth control method.)

CONS: The copper IUD may cause more cramping and heavier periods. If you're on a tight budget, you might find the cost of an IUD prohibitive—about $600 to $700 for the device and doctor's fees for insertion. (Not all insurance companies cover IUDs, so check with yours first.) Many women are afraid of IUDs because of reports about the dangers of early IUDs. These are based on the Dalkon Shield, an IUD that has been off the market for about twenty years and that caused a lot of reproductive problems for women. However, today's T-shaped IUDs are much safer and more effective, says Mitchell Creinin, M.D., an associate professor and director of family planning at the University of Pittsburgh.

RELIABILITY: Because both IUDs are long-term birth control methods, doctors base how reliable they are over the long term. Therefore, the copper IUD is 98 percent effective over ten years. Mirena is more than 99 percent effective over five years—that is, in a five-year period, less than 1 percent of users became pregnant.

Norplant

Six matchstick-sized implants are inserted into the upper arm and then slowly release the hormone progesterone, which inhibits ovulation.

PROS: Norplant lasts for five years.

CONS: Like Depo-Provera, the hormones in Norplant may cause you to gain weight. If you have a low pain threshold, you may not like that the insertion of Norplant is considered a surgical procedure, albeit an outpatient one. Also, you may scar at the insertion site. Norplant can be pricey—and not covered by insurance, depending on your carrier. Expect to shell out up to $800 for an initial exam, the product itself, and the insertion procedure.

RELIABILITY: Approximately 99.9 percent.

The Pill

There are two kinds of Pills. The traditional Pill is a combination of hormones estrogen and progesterone. The minipill is just progesterone. According to Planned Parenthood, only the traditional Pill, with

> **Wedding Wisdom**
> *We had discussed before that we were not looking to have kids for at least five years, so we decided that the Pill would be our easiest and safest method of birth control. And since I knew my skin tends to break out when I am under pressure, the doctor prescribed me a Pill that also clears up the skin.*
>
> AMY, TEXAS

its estrogen-progesterone combination, fully inhibits ovulation. Otherwise, both kinds of birth control pills also make the cervical mucus thick so sperm can't travel well in it and thin the uterine lining so that implantation of a fertilized egg is nearly impossible.

PROS: Women who choose to take the Pill may find that their periods are lighter, come with fewer menstrual cramps, and any irregularities in their cycle disappear. In addition, for some women, the Pill may alleviate certain PMS (premenstrual syndrome) symptoms and clear up acne.

> **Wedding Wisdom**
> *I saw my gynecologist and got a bunch of refills on my birth control pills before the wedding. I was moving across the country after my wedding and didn't know when I could get refills once I got there.*
> SHARAYU, OREGON

CONS: If you don't remember to take your Pill every day and at the same time each day, you increase the risk of pregnancy. So, if you tend to be forgetful or already have too much on your plate to keep track of taking a daily pill, this birth control method may not be your best choice. Also, pills average about twenty-five dollars per month, and not all insurance companies cover their purchase. So, the cost can add up for a couple on a budget.

RELIABILITY: 99 percent for both kinds of Pills, as long as they're taken on a regular schedule. Any deviation from that schedule, though, decreases the Pill's efficacy.

Other Birth Control Options

Abstinence
If you're waiting until you're married to have intercourse, this is, in essence, your only birth control option.

Pros: There is no cost, doctor's visits, or artificial hormones involved.

Cons: It may be tough to forego intercourse, especially if you two are somewhat sexually active.

Reliability: 100 percent, as long as there is no genital-to-genital contact. Otherwise, you are risking pregnancy.

Natural Family Planning

The so-called rhythm, or "fertility awareness," method relies on charting of a woman's body temperature and checking her cervical mucus to determine when she is ovulating. Then she and her partner abstain from sex on the "unsafe" days. This requires diligence on the woman's part to check and chart her temperature and cervical mucus daily plus keep track of her menstrual periods.

Pros: Couples whose religion prevents them from using hormonal or barrier contraception prefer this "natural" method. Also, because temperature and cervical changes signal ovulation, women who are well versed in their body's own fertility signs may have an easier time getting pregnant down the road. That's because they'll know when they're ovulating and can time intercourse accordingly.

Cons: Women with irregular menstrual periods may have a hard time using this method. Also, learning to chart your "fertility awareness" requires some schooling, so this can be a time-consuming method. Finally, some women may feel uncomfortable with the notion of checking their own cervical mucus or daily discharge.

Reliability: Planned Parenthood reports reliability rates that vary from 75 percent to 99 percent effective.

THE DOCTOR (OR NURSE OR MIDWIFE) IS IN

With all this talk of making babies or preventing babies from being made, there is one important issue that you still need to consider: *which* medical practitioner you will go to see for your women's health care. Most women assume that a gynecologist is their only option, but that's no longer true. There are a number of other kinds of doctors and nurses who can do a fine job of providing gynecologic treatment, preconception counseling, and your pre- and post-partum care. In fact, there are several issues to consider when choosing a women's health-care practitioner: Do you like this person and his or her bedside manner? Does your insurance cover his or her practice? And, most important, does this person specialize in women's health?

"A woman spends half her life in her reproductive years, trying to avoid pregnancy, and the majority of women need time to talk about their family-planning needs," says Dr. Creinin, a family planning specialist at the University of Pittsburgh. That's why the person you want counseling you on your birth control options and other issues related specifically to women's health should be as up-to-date as possible on both of these topics. "For example, there is a conference on contraceptive technologies every year, and I'd want to know if this particular practitioner has attended each year," says Dr. Creinin, who also suggests asking how the practitioner stays current on information. "I'm a general obstetrician and gynecologist, and I've had basic training in contraception, but what I learned in school is relatively inadequate." That's why quizzing a doctor or nurse practitioner on his or her continuing education efforts is simply good medicine.

Following are brief explanations of the most common kinds of health practitioners that you may want to consider for your gynecologic care.

Certified Nurse Midwife

Don't let the name *midwife* fool you into thinking that these health practitioners are laypeople. In fact, they are highly trained individuals—usually registered nurses who've spent extra years training in nursing, women's health care, and midwifery—and, according to the American College of Nurse Midwifery, most certified nurse midwives work in hospital settings or in doctor's offices. They can provide primary care to any woman in her childbearing years, whether she's planning on having children now, in the near future, or never. In addition, certified nurse midwives are trained in prenatal care, labor, and delivery and are the primary practitioner at many hospital and home births across the country.

For example, at the University of Michigan Medical Center where I gave birth to my two daughters, I received all of my obstetrical care from a certified nurse midwife. This hospital believed that women with high-risk pregnancies (i.e., carrying multiples), or potentially dangerous medical conditions such as gestational diabetes, should see medical doctors. All other women with normal pregnancies would receive excellent care from a certified nurse midwife, who usually had more time to see patients than a doctor would—thirty minutes or more versus fifteen minutes for doctors.

Family Physician

A doctor in a family practice is usually a generalist who is equipped to treat everyone—from children to the elderly. Some people choose a family physician for the adults and children in the family so that they can get all of their care under one roof. And just because a family physician treats all ages doesn't mean he or she may not be the right doctor for you. If you find out that a certain family physician spends a lot of time on women's health issues, then that's a good sign. However, "if the doctor is more interested in pediatrics," warns Dr. Creinin, "then that's not a good person to see for contraception." Despite extensive training in women's health care, a family physician is likely to refer a pregnant patient to a certified nurse midwife or obstetrician.

Gynecologist/Obstetrician

This kind of doctor has received extensive training in women's health and necessary care during pregnancy, although some gynecologists do not work as obstetricians. So, if you're considering seeing a gynecologist—and want to start a family in the near future—make sure you determine upfront if your gynecologist will be able and willing to care for you throughout your pregnancy and delivery. Otherwise, you'll need to be referred to another doctor, either in the practice or somewhere else entirely. Again, even though this doctor calls him- or herself a gynecologist and/or obstetrician, "it's patient beware," says Dr. Creinin. "How much is this doctor interested in keeping up with things and what kind of training did this doctor get for contraception?" Don't let the doctor title fool you: you still need to investigate how well this doctor's training, background, and knowledge meshes with your needs before agreeing to be his or her patient.

Internal Medicine Doctor

Like the family physician, an internal medicine doctor, or internist, tends to be a generalist and is often designated as a "primary-care physician" by an insurance company. Plenty of internists, however, have received additional training in gynecology and obstetrics and therefore specialize in women's health. But it's not uncommon for an internist to refer a pregnant patient to a specialist, like an obstetrician or certified nurse midwife.

Nurse Practitioner

A nurse practitioner who has an interest in women's health may also be called a family planning nurse practitioner. Like a certified nurse midwife, she has had extra training in the women's health area, and she usually works side-by-side with the doctor in a doctor's practice. A nurse practitioner can also see patients on her own to do pelvic exams, take pap smears, discuss family planning options, and even to write prescriptions. When a patient becomes pregnant, she'll need to send her to an obstetrician or certified nurse midwife for her continued care during pregnancy.

Physician Assistant

Physician assistants, or PAs, are another option to consider for women's health practitioners. Like certified nurse midwives, PAs are often employed in practices with medical doctors but are as qualified to see and treat patients as doctors are. In fact, a recent survey from the American Academy of Physician Assistants, the organization that licenses PAs, reported that nearly four in ten physician assistants worked in a group physician office and that 81 percent of them focused on OB-GYN patients exclusively. Physician assistants can perform comprehensive gynecological exams, prescribe birth control, and treat pregnant women, including attending the birth of a child.

BALANCE: THE BOTTOM LINE

It may seem strange to consider family planning a part of your wedding plans, but it is a critical element in your overall state of balance. Why? Because before you say, "I do," you and your fiancé first must determine if you want children at all and, if so, when. Unless you anticipate starting a family right away, you two will need to determine the best birth control plan for your future family. This chapter has given you a thorough rundown on the most common birth control methods available, including over-the-counter, prescription, and natural options.

In addition, regardless of when you plan to become parents (if at all), you'll need to decide if the medical practitioner who takes care of you and your birth control needs is the best person for the job. Is he or she well versed in the latest birth control methods? Is he or she available for prenatal care should you become pregnant? These issues should not be left until the honeymoon when you may be having intercourse for the first time, or, worse yet, the day you discover that you've missed your period and a home pregnancy test comes up positive. Figure out your family planning ahead of time to ensure a happy family life after the wedding.

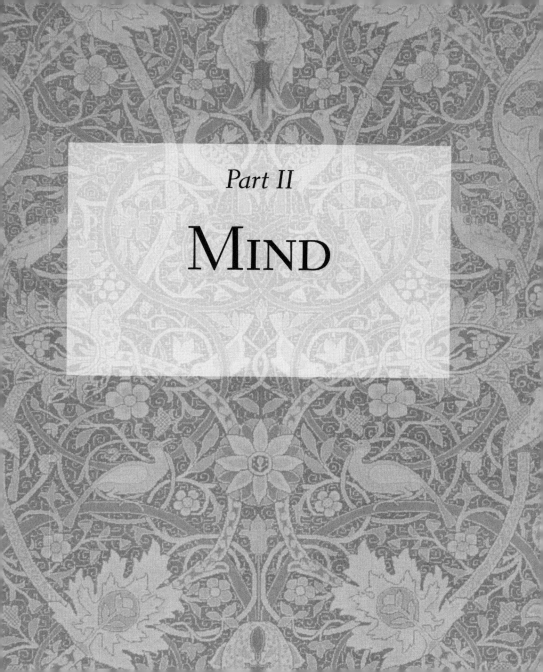

Part II

MIND

5

WHO ARE YOU AND WHO ARE YOU BECOMING?

IF YOU'RE ANYTHING like me, you couldn't wait to get married. The idea of being off the dating scene and in a stable, monogamous relationship was just about as close to heaven as I could imagine—and marriage has been all that and more. But I know that despite my excitement about getting engaged and planning my wedding, there were times during the prewedding period and afterward as well when the reality of what was happening in my life hit me.

I wouldn't say that I panicked when I had these reality moments, but they did give me pause and cause me to reflect on where I'd come from, where I was now, and where I was going in the future as a married person. And it was weird. One of the biggest changes I had to adjust to—and you will, too—is going from thinking as "I" to "we." That's not to say that you lose your total sense of "I" when you get married. Rather, because you are beholden to someone, you must consider that person's feelings as you plan everything in your life—from what you'll get at the supermarket to when and where you'll take a vacation. This slight adjustment in how you plan your weekends, job choices, and even your social calendar can take some getting used to—especially if you've been single for many years and are used to doing things on your own terms only. But it's also critical that you anticipate making this psychological transition from single person to married woman, or your relationship may encounter rocky times.

I know a man and woman who were madly in love, and, like most madly in love couples, they got married. Only problem was, even though they became husband and wife, they continued to live veritably separate lives. Yes, they shared a home and expenses, but she continued to make career choices without consulting her husband first, and he planned his social calendar without her input. Although their marriage may be an extreme example, their outcome was also extreme—they never made it to their two-year anniversary, ending up in divorce court instead.

I don't mean to scare you with this story, but I do want you to think about it as you make your transition from Ms. to Mrs., and here's why: as I said before, once you agree to marry someone, you must start thinking in terms of "we." That's not to say that you can't continue to think of "I," but you can't do it at the expense of "we."

"You're going to have to fit into three roles once you get married, and you must be prepared to do so," says Anthony Jurich, Ph.D., a marriage and family therapy expert at Kansas State University in Manhattan, Kansas. "Your first role is still as an individual, and you don't give that up when you slip on a ring and say, 'I do.' You're still your own person, you still have freedom of choice, and you're still autonomous." But on the flip side, now you're also part of a partnership, and that partnership—your second role—means that you now have another person who has needs, wants, and desires that must be considered and accommodated. So, that's part of your partnership identity. The third identity or role, like it or not, is with those who will think of you simply as your husband's wife—him plus an "appendage." Conversely, your husband will be the appendage when dealing with your colleagues or those who know you well but not your husband. Together, they make up your three identities or roles you'll play in married life.

DEFINING WHO YOU ARE

Chances are that you already know who *you* are—how you define yourself, what you like to do in your spare time, what career you've chosen. Of the three roles that you must play in married life, this is the one that is probably the clearest in your mind. The appendage role, as crudely defined earlier, is one that you and your husband will probably only have to deal with on an occasional basis when you or your husband's work life and married life collide, and it's a role I wouldn't spend too much time worrying about. However, if there's one role that you'll need to spend time nurturing in the early years of your relationship and married life, it's that partnership role.

"What I get too often is the wife sits there and says, 'I'm a Democrat,' and the husband replies, 'I'm a Republican,' and there is no dual-ness and no we-ness in how they talk about their partnership," says Dr. Jurich. In fact, there doesn't seem to be a partnership at all. To define and develop your partnership, you need to have things that you share. "It's OK to say, 'The garage is his because he has his tools there, and I have the kitchen because I like to cook, but the den is ours because we like watching TV together.' There's the element of what's 'you' and what's 'him' and what's 'us.'"

Another example of good "we-ness" is looking more at *how* you talk about what you like to do together, rather than *what* you do together only, says Dr. Jurich. If you say, "We like to travel, we enjoy going to the theater together, and we're both Christians," yes, you've identified what you have in common, but look how you've presented it—as "we." You could also say the same thing as, "She likes to travel and so do I," but do you see how un-*we* that sounds? Sure, you like the same things but you haven't presented the information in a couple-defined way. Once talking in the "we" becomes second nature, you'll know you're on the right path to solidifying your partnership role.

Identity Exercise

To be honest, figuring out who you are as a couple will be a work in progress, and once you're aware of its amorphous nature, you won't stress out too much over it. To get started on developing that identity, though, here is an exercise that Dr. Jurich suggests you do with your fiancé. It should help you uncover any preconceived notions of how he defines himself and how he may apply those definitions to your partnership identity—and the roles you each play in your marriage. Once you have this information, you can use it, along with your own definitions of identity, to help figure out who you two are going to be as a couple. This exercise uses a sports metaphor, so that should go over well with any sports-loving fiancé. Here's what you should do:

Go up to your fiancé and say, "Honey, I want to play a game of ball with you. What do we need?" Now, your fiancé is going to do one of two things in response. One, he's either going to define what his idea of "playing ball" is by saying, "I'll bring the football, and we'll throw it around" or "I'll get my glove." Or, two, he's going to look to you for input by saying something like, "I'll get the equipment, but first, what kind of ball do you want to play?"

If your fiancé answers in the former manner, you'll need to point out the obvious discrepancies: "What makes you think I said football or baseball?" The preferred response is the latter one, where when you lob such a general suggestion in your fiancé's direction, he should hit a home run by responding with a clarifying question. Despite the seemingly trivial nature of discussing playing ball, this is an excellent example of how two people can come together to figure out what is best for both of them rather than just going with what one person likes.

"Think about it this way," adds Dr. Jurich. "You and I have agreed to get married. I want to know what kind of marriage you want, so I ask you just this. Then I tell you the kind of relationship I want us to have. Once you hear what I have to say, you can respond with, 'This is what I don't want,' and then you go from there."

If the sports metaphor exercise isn't revealing enough, make a date with each other to talk about these "what do you want from our marriage" issues. Tell him that you'll bring over Chinese takeout or pizza, and together you'll sit down and talk about all of the traits and characteristics that you expect of one another and that will define you in your marriage. For example, if you discover that he expects you to do all the housework because he defines that as women's work, you need to figure out if that task fits in with your idea of what a wife's role should be. If not, then you'll need to discuss how you can make such a seemingly mundane task fit in with your couple identity.

I'm sure it may seem silly to discuss who will be cleaning the bathrooms or doing the laundry once you get married, especially with all of the more pressing issues you have with your upcoming wedding. But remember: if you were in the market for a car, you'd do the research up front. You'd list the features you're looking for, get all the specs on the car, and even look under the hood. Well, these exercises in defining who you are, who you will be in your marriage, and what roles you'll each play are pretty much the same thing as what you'd do before buying a car.

"If your fiancé isn't amenable to this kind of discussion, you need to ask him, 'Why are you willing to marry me without talking about all of this stuff? Am I not worthy of this? If you're telling me that I'm less worthy than buying a car, then we need to sit down and talk about this,'" says Dr. Jurich. In addition, if you're the one holding back on having this talk, you need to figure out why.

Making a List

Once you've convinced your fiancé or yourself of the need for this exercise, give it another go. Tell him that you should each take a week so you can come up with a separate list of how you are going to define who you are as a couple or to jot down the things that you like to do, ideally as a couple, and that you hope to continue doing in married life. (Remember: just because you're getting married that doesn't mean that you have to lose your sense of self.)

Figuring out what you're going to put on your list may actually be easier than you think, simply because similarities are probably what brought and have kept you together—and are simmering below the surface. In addition, this exercise will be empowering for you as a couple to say, "We are going to do this together." In the midst of all the craziness of planning your wedding, it may be refreshing as well.

To keep things light, Jurich suggests shooting for a David Letterman–like "Top 10 List," such as "The Top 10 Things Sue and Mike Enjoy Doing Together—and for Which They Won't Get Arrested—Are . . ." Don't put too much pressure on yourselves to put these ideas in ranking order. Just get them down on paper.

COMPATIBILITY AND COMPROMISE

Once you have your lists down on paper, compare them. If you agree on everything, that's great. But it's probably not likely. So, you're going to have to look at all the stuff you've put down and divide it into three categories.

"The stuff where you're the same is no sweat," advises Dr. Jurich. "Next there is the stuff you can compromise on. If your fiancé says that he wants to continue playing softball five days a week and he wants you to come and watch him at all five games, you might think that five games a week is too much for you to handle. So, you can respond by saying, 'I'll go two nights, but weekends are too much for me.' By saying that you're willing to be a softball widow some of the time, you're also making it clear to your fiancé that if he is going to make playing softball such a priority, he's going to have to be a softball bachelor some of the time as well. It also gives him something to think about; you've given him your consent to continue pursuing his hobbies, but he needs to decide if being away from his wife for the sake of his hobby so much during the week is worth it. So, he may come back and say, 'I don't want to miss out on weekends with you. Why don't I limit my softball to three weeknights only, and you'll try to come to two of those games?' Now you're compromising."

Although that's a nice example of a simple solution to a situation, sometimes compromise doesn't come that easily. If your or your fiancé's list includes something that is beyond your imagination, then you're really going to have to work on finding a way to negotiate it.

If you're faced with an idea that seems way out there—such as his suggestion that you eat out every night—keep the following in mind: why does he need this, and how can we deal with these needs in a compatible manner? For example, his desire to eat out could be his way of avoiding telling you that you're a terrible cook, but sooner or later that truth needs to come out. Instead of breaking your budget and appeasing him with his restaurant-only policy, talk about *why* he wants to eat out. Then, if you determine that subpar cooking is to blame, you can make signing up for a cooking class together part of your solution.

Of course, there is a worst-case scenario to this list-making exercise: when you come up against something that is truly incompatible, says Dr. Jurich. "If you sit down and say, 'Honey, that's not something I can do,' and ask, 'How important is this for you?' and even then you can't seem to find a compromise, then you need to call in a counselor."

One area where you might find yourselves incompatible is on the issue of whether or not you're going to change your name. In my experience, it is usually the man in the relationship who has a set idea about his wife taking his name, and in some cases there's no changing his mind. Although I support a woman's right to choose to

---

Wedding Wisdom

When my husband and I got married, I had just started a business that had my last name in it. It didn't make sense to change my name, and my husband didn't mind. I found that others had a really hard time with my decision, though. One of my company's vendors asked what he should call me now that I was married, and I told him to call me what he'd always called me—Gwen. "Just Gwen?" he replied. "You mean like Cher or Madonna?" My husband and I had a good laugh over that one.

GWEN, NEW JERSEY

change or keep her name, I don't believe she should do so under duress, nor should her husband browbeat her into making a name-change decision that only he prefers.

I have a friend who was on the fence about changing her name throughout her engagement. As a young writer in the publishing world, she'd started to get established under her maiden name and was hoping to continue that momentum by keeping her maiden name after marriage, at least professionally. Then there were her conflicting feelings of wanting to feel like a family by having the same last name as her husband and, should they have them, any future children. Despite her uncertainty, her fiancé couldn't offer her any support during her quandary because he couldn't see things from her perspective. Where he came from, women changed their names once they got married, and that's that. Although she attempted to discuss the issue with him, he refused. Not wanting to call off the wedding over the issue, this friend finally relented. "He was so upset at the time that I just decided to do it for him and to learn to live with his last name," she told me.

Believe it or not, how your fiancé reacts to your name-change decision can say a lot about him and how he'll be when other sticky situations come up throughout your relationship. "If he's going to be rigid about the name issue, what else is he going to be rigid about?" Dr. Jurich asks.

> ### Wedding Wisdom
> *Since my first name is Jenny, and it is very common among my group of friends, people have always called me by my last name. So changing my name was a hard thing for me to do, but I felt that it was necessary because I did not want to have a different last name from my husband or children. For my wedding present, my husband gave me a personalized license plate for my car with my maiden name on it. For some reason, that gift made me feel better about the whole thing.*
>
> JENNY, NEW YORK

When you come to an impasse like my friend did, someone is simply going to have to give in—unless this is a relationship-ending impasse. If you've gotten to the point of agreeing to get married, it probably won't be. So, if you find yourself giving in and changing your name, for example, don't just succumb quietly. Dr. Jurich suggests letting your fiancé know that you're making a big sacrifice for him. Although life isn't a big game of scorekeeping, when it comes down to it, he owes you. "Tell him that the next time you come to an impasse like you did with the name-change thing," he says, "he's going to have to be the one who gives in."

> **Wedding Wisdom**
> *I added his name to mine, kept my maiden name as my middle name, and try to make a point of using the three names when I introduce myself, but sometimes I forget.*
> MELISSA, PENNSYLVANIA

Of course, this sets up a scenario of conditional give-and-take, which I suggest you avoid over the long term. However, if you do end up making a big sacrifice, such as with your name or the decision not to have kids, you need to let your partner know of the scope of the decision and that such decisions can't always be so one-sided, with only one person giving in. It's got to be equal.

THE NAME-CHANGE GAME

Of course, my friend's name-change situation is less than ideal. I think that the optimal way for any couple to approach this topic is to think of the bride's feelings first and the groom's feelings second. Remember: traditionally, it is the bride who changes her name (originally as a sign of the transfer of property ownership), and she is the one who must deal with all the administrative hassles plus the social and psychological adjustment that goes along with changing a name.

Now, if her future husband doesn't recognize all that goes into the name-change game and won't give her the freedom to weigh the pros and cons of a name change, perhaps *he* should consider changing his name to hers, even for a few minutes; that exercise ought to give him a more realistic idea of the task that lies ahead for his future wife. Finally, if you must consider others' opinions on the topic, such as family members, weigh them last.

Let me offer some full disclosure before completely delving into the topic of what to do with your name after you get married. When I was dating, I was one of those

> **Wedding Wisdom**
> *I am a little sentimental about changing my last name, but it means a lot to me to have the same name as my husband-to-be and my kids-to-be.*
>
> Terez, New York

women who always tried on her boyfriends' last names. If his name sounded good with mine, then I thought that maybe we had a future together. Of course, this is a silly way of judging a relationship, but I'm sure most women (even the most modern thinking among us) have done this at one time or another. So, considering my past promiscuousness of trying on men's names, it seemed a no-brainer for me to simply change my name to my husband's when we got married. In fact, I just assumed I'd become a three-named person after marriage, using my first name, my maiden name as my middle name, and my married name at the end. As a published author, I figured I'd seamlessly make this transition with my byline and books, but that was not to be so. A funny thing happened on the way to my name change, and it all started the day we applied for our marriage license.

My husband, Bill, and I were married in New York State, and the day we went to the marriage license bureau, there was a very long line. After completing our marriage license application, we waited with the other nervous engaged couples. Because it was a slow-moving line, all of us had a lot of time to talk. It was a jovial crowd, and many of those in line with us remarked at how easy it was in New York State for a person to change his or her name when getting married. I say his or her because our marriage license application had a line on which each of us could write "new surname." Bill was joking with the others in line that all of us should change our name to Lightfoot or something kooky, just to cause a blip in that day's demographics. But his brevity about the name-change issue really hit home with me.

Although I'd written in Bill's last name as my new surname on the application (and he'd written nothing), the finality of what I was about to do dawned on me. Then I wondered: was I really prepared to take his name? Although I did end up keeping his surname on our marriage license, I never got used to the idea of being a three-named person, especially as people increasingly dropped Ingram in favor of my married name. In social situations, I reverted to introducing myself as Leah Ingram, and so did Bill. In the end, I never fully changed my name. Sure, my marriage license has my married surname on it, but I never followed through and changed my name on my social security card and my passport—two legal documents where name changes are a must. So, as far as the U.S. government, including the Internal

---

Wedding Wisdom

I agonized over the name change for professional reasons and then determined that it was more important for me to have consistency and one identity. Other than taking a lot of paperwork and phone calls to change my name on documents, credit cards, etc., it was worth it for me to take my husband's much shorter, easier-to-spell name.

JUDY, NEW JERSEY

Revenue Service, is concerned, I'm still Leah Ingram, and I always will be. In fact, my husband has gotten to the point where he doesn't think women should automatically change their name when married. "I don't have the guts to change my name to my wife's," he jokes. "Why should she have to change hers to mine?"

As a postscript to my name-change story, you may be wondering what happened when we had kids and how I dealt with the issue of having a different last name from my children. Well, at Bill's insistence, we gave each girl Ingram as a middle name, so that they will always feel connected to me. In addition, I've mellowed to the fact that when it comes to my children's friends, they are going to call me by my married name. They simply assume that I have the same last name as my kids, so when they call me Mrs. I'm OK with that.

> **Wedding Wisdom**
> *My fiancé had always imagined that his future wife would be proud to bear his name, and I also knew that I would be thrilled and honored to change my last name to that of the man I love to show we are truly one. Plus, it sure helped that I have a long and cumbersome last name and his is short and easy!*
> SARAH, ILLINOIS

Married Name Options

Now that you know how I handled (or mishandled, depending on how you see it) the name issue, let's address the issue of how you're going to deal with your name after you're married. Like most of the important stuff in marriage, this is something you need to think about and discuss well in advance of your wedding. Don't do as I did and end up making your name decision while waiting in line for your marriage license. Give yourself ample time to think this through. Here are four name-changing or name-keeping scenarios and the pros and cons of each.

Changing Your Name

This situation is right for you if you're a traditional person who believes that taking your husband's name after marriage is simply the right thing to do. I know a woman who sees the adoption of her husband's name as one of her greatest accomplishments: she's proud to say that she's someone's wife, and it's terrific that the title is so important to her. Changing your name also makes sense if you want to have continuity with any future children or if sharing a name will give you a greater sense of being a family. I know plenty of women who hated their maiden names—either because of the way they sounded or the unhappy memories they represented—and couldn't wait to change their names.

One cautionary note: if you're planning on changing your name for social reasons but keeping your maiden name professionally, understand that this task is harder to pull off than it appears. I have one friend who did just that, and years later she's still grappling with her identity. "When I pick up the phone to call someone, I always have to stop and remind myself who I am at that moment. Am I Mrs. Smith calling my son's school, or am I Ms. Jones, the professional, calling a colleague?" she told me. Even after being married for twelve years, she still hasn't grown used to wearing two name hats.

> **Wedding Wisdom**
>
> *One of the big issues my fiancé and I have had is my name change. I am a very independent person, plus my name means a lot for my career. I'm a television reporter, and viewers identify with my name. But it means a lot to my fiancé for me to take his name, in both public and private. I finally decided it's a small battle I could concede to for the sake of marital harmony.*
>
> ANNE, IOWA

Keeping Your Maiden Name

Obviously, this is the scenario I favor because it works for me. It also tends to work well for professional women who are older and established in their careers. If you're considering keeping your maiden name, make sure you speak to other women who've done the same. Ask them about how they've handled many of the name-related issues that have given me pause over the years, such as coming to terms with the fact that you won't have the same last name as your children. Talk these over with your fiancé and really spend some time getting comfortable with these and other notions related to keeping your name.

If you can't handle the idea of not sharing a last name with your kids, then you and your future husband need to discuss other name options, such as your changing your name to his for continuity's sake (the obvious); giving the children your last name instead of his (then he'll have those name issues to deal with and that you'll have to discuss); or choosing an entirely different name for you and your family.

What I suggest you avoid, however, is splitting names within your family—that is, keeping your name but giving some of your children your last name and some your husband's last name. This may seem like a good idea in theory, but it can be too confusing for young siblings. You're a grown-up, and you have the wisdom and maturity to understand why you may have a different name from some of your

---

Wedding Wisdom

At this point, I think I've settled on using my maiden name as my middle name. That way I can leave it out if I want or need to keep my name short, but I can always use it if I want to, too. As for the kids, we've come to a compromise. Our first son will get my maiden name as his first name and the next will get my mother's maiden name. If we have girls we'll work the names into their middle names somehow. So even if no one else knows, my family heritage will be intertwined with our children's names.

LEAH, MASSACHUSETTS

children, but your children don't. So, don't confuse the issue further by giving them differing names. (I think the same rule should be applied in families where the mother and father have different religions. One kid shouldn't be Jewish and the other Christian, if those are the parents' religions. Turn to Chapter 10, "Religion and Your Future Family," for more on that topic.)

Hyphenating Your Name

In a vacuum, it seems like the best option to have one or both of you change your names to a name that includes both of your original names. But, in reality, this is a really terrible alternative, especially if children will be involved and will be receiving this hyphenated last name as their own. "When it comes to hyphenated names, you've got to think long term," warns Daylle Deanna Schwartz, a relationship expert and author of several books, including *How to Please a Woman in and out of Bed* (Adams, 2000). "I'm curious to see the next generation of children with hyphenated names, who grow up and marry someone with hyphenated names.

Wedding Wisdom

I'm a feminist and didn't want to change my name. Plus, I was divorced and had to go through the enormous pain of changing it when I'd first gotten married and then changing it back to my maiden name after the divorce. I just didn't want the hassle. My husband is very traditional and was very hurt that I didn't want to take his name. We compromised by me hyphenating my name (I'd suggested that we both hyphenate but he wasn't having any of that). However, were I to do it again, I wouldn't change my legal name.

KELLY, ILLINOIS

Well, what if they choose to hyphenate their married name?" This may seem like a ridiculous example, but with so many families choosing hyphenated names for their children, this issue will probably become a reality in the next few decades, so seriously consider the ramifications of your hyphenated name decision.

Of course, you, the woman, could choose to hyphenate your name only, so that you still feel connected to your maiden name yet you're also using your married name. Your kids can get your husband's name only. There are plenty of women who've hyphenated on paper, such as Sue Smith-Jones, but continue to call themselves Sue Smith, because that's what they're used to. If that works for you, then do it.

Choosing a New Family Name

I know a couple in Florida who couldn't agree on whether she should take his name or he should take hers, but they knew that they wanted to be known by the same family name after they were married. So, what did they do? Combined their last names to make a new name that they would each adopt. That way they would go through the whole name-change process together, including the mourning of the loss of their old, single self, which is perfectly normal for anyone changing his or her name to experience. Here's the catch, though: because this couple expected that they'd get flack from their families about their name decision and didn't want to add that element to their already stressful wedding plans, they didn't announce their new name at their wedding, reception, or on their invitations. "We'd instructed

> **Wedding Wisdom**
> *I worried that my first name didn't sound good with my fiancé's last name, but in the end it wasn't about how it sounded or whether I was giving anything up, but that we were going to start a family. What is the most basic thing that a family always has in common? Its last name.*
>
> SARA, NEW YORK

the officiant and the deejay to introduce us as 'the bride and groom, Jennifer and John,' rather than Mrs. and Mr.," Jennifer recalls. (By the way, this approach works well when the bride is keeping her name and doesn't feel comfortable being introduced as Mrs. Smith after her wedding ceremony and at her reception.) Rather, they ordered thank-you notes with their new name on them, and included an explanation for the name change in each note they sent. The end result? Some raised eyebrows for sure, but, overall, their family and friends supported their decision.

Widespread Surnames

Perhaps your maiden name is an uncommon one that is difficult to spell and even harder to pronounce. For you the notion of changing your name after marriage might be somewhat attractive. Well, if you're looking to adopt a common surname—either by taking your husband's or creating a new name for both of you—consider this list of the most common last names in America, according to the most recent U.S. Census Bureau statistics on the website census.gov.

1. Smith
2. Johnson
3. Williams
4. Jones
5. Brown
6. Davis
7. Miller
8. Wilson
9. Moore
10. Taylor

Friendships After the Wedding

I'm sure your and your fiancé's friends have been great pillars of support for both of you as you plan your wedding. I know that I couldn't have gotten through my wedding plans had it not been for the unquestioned devotion of my closest girlfriends, and I'm sure Bill felt the same about his guy friends. Yes, we were there for each other a lot as well, but there were certain issues that I only felt comfortable discussing with girlfriends, and I'm so glad they were around for me.

Although I encourage you to continue to nurture those friendships after you get married, please understand that just by the nature of your now being a married person, those relationships are bound to change, and you'll need to work harder at maintaining them. Likewise, now that you and your fiancé will have adopted the persona of husband and wife, it is critical that you work at developing couple-only friendships with other husbands and wives. This last part of this chapter is devoted to friendships and how you can maintain them, develop them, or let them go after you're married.

Old Friends

Earlier in this chapter I discussed the importance of "I" in a relationship. A great way to maintain your "I" is through the friends who've known you from before you got together with your fiancé. These could be your childhood chums, your sorority sisters, or the girls from work with whom you go out for drinks occasionally. These women are an important part of your life, and you need to make that clear to not only yourself, but to your fiancé and them as well. It's so easy for friends to have feelings of jealousy as you spend more time with your fiancé and then husband, so let them know that they are dear to you by making plans to see them on a regular basis. In addition, you need to make it clear to your fiancé the place these female friendships have in your heart and mind. "You want to be a whole person in your relationship, and part of that involves maintaining your own friendships," says Schwartz. "It is totally OK to get together with girlfriends, just as it's OK for your fiancé to get together with his guy friends. The key is having a level of trust."

Schwartz recalls a newly married woman she knows who went out to a jazz club one evening after work with her girlfriends. "The whole time she was there she was so nervous. She was worried that she was going to bump into [her husband], and that he would be so jealous if he knew she was out at a bar," she says. "I asked her if her husband goes out to bars with his friends, and she said he did. 'But that's what guys do,' her friend replied."

Issues of friendship revolve around communication, as do so many things in a relationship. If you don't talk about your expectations of how you'll maintain your individual friendships after you're married, then that lack of communication will lead to unanswered questions and the erosion of trust. "You need to say things like, 'I'd like you to feel free to go out with your friends, and I want to feel free to do the same. The only thing I ask is that we are respectful of one another and let each other know of these plans in advance,'" advises Schwartz.

One caveat to the old and separate friends rule is when those relationships could sabotage a marriage. I know of too many women whose girlfriends were jealous of a bride-to-be's engaged state. So, every time they would get together, those friends would talk negatively about the woman's fiancé or the foundation of marriage in general. With friends like these, you need to let them know that what they're saying is hurtful and upsetting, and that if they don't stop, you'll have to stop seeing them.

In fact, one of the hardest things about old friends and new marriages is letting go of friendships that have run their course. Too many people try to resuscitate relationships with old friends that have simply run out of life. If you find that you have nothing in common or nothing to say to an old friend, or even if you simply don't enjoy being around someone anymore, you must let that friendship go. Maybe you're the one who has been guilty of dragging the relationship along, in that you're the primary scheduler of events. If so, don't call this friend for a few months and see what happens. If you gradually fall out of touch, then it was meant to be. However, if you find yourself always on the receiving end of invitations from someone you'd rather not socialize with anymore, I'd suggest writing her a note to tell her so. Write that although you've enjoyed her friendship over the years, you feel as if you've grown apart, and there is nothing left to sustain the relationship. Therefore, you think it's best if you don't see one another anymore. Yes, this sounds very much like a break-up letter, and I guess that's what it is. Close your note by wishing her well, and send it off. It won't be easy, but it's necessary.

New, Couple-Centered Friends

In the best of all worlds, you and your fiancé's old friends will get married, and you can all move forward in your friendships as couples as opposed to single people tagging along with a couple. I know this has happened with many of Bill and my friends over the years. It's been a great way for all of us to stay in touch and stay current, because we are all going through so many of the same transitions at the same time—getting married, buying a home, having children, and so forth. I only hope you're as lucky.

What's great about having other couple friends is it really cements your relationship and validates who you are as a couple—

important elements to have, especially after you're first married. It all goes back to the we-ness that every couple should aspire to create in their marriage. Who you choose as your friends are part of the answer to the question, "Who are we as a couple?"

You'll find the answer to this question—and potential couple friends—by pursuing certain activities together. For example, I know a couple who've had the same Tuesday night couple's tennis game for ten years. Through their devotion to playing couple's tennis, they've met and become friends with numerous husbands and wives who share their love of the game. So, as you do fun things together, like joining a softball league or volunteering at a soup kitchen, look for other couples doing the same and see if you can strike up a conversation.

Funny thing is, when you make the conscious decision to cultivate couples friendships, it's going to feel a lot like dating all over again. And I guess in a certain sense, it's the same thing. So, if you know a few couples who seem like they would be fun to get to know and hang out with, start by figuring out which of these couples you want to target. Ask each other, "Well, what kind of people do we want to be friends with?" and list the qualities you enjoy in your friends. Then, try to match them with the people you know. If you find a couple that fits the bill, invite them over for a meal or out to a restaurant. "One couple invites another couple out, you sit down, you talk, and you see if you have things in common," says Dr. Jurich, who stresses that what you're looking for in common are things that are "couplecentric," not traits that are focused on individuals. So, if two of the four of you work as lawyers, that might be nice, but it won't cement a friendship. But if you discover that you all attend the same house of worship, well, that's a step in the right direction. This way, you know that you probably have a similar belief and value system—and that you'll be able to see each other at least once a week at worship and at other religious functions.

Once you've had success cultivating a couple friendship, you and your fiancé will need to determine how many such friendships you'll be able to balance. With family and single friends, plus your respective careers tugging you in different directions, you don't want to be too promiscuous in your search for couple friends: it's not fair to anyone involved. Friendships are important, but having enough time during your week to spend with each other should be your top priority in the end.

BALANCE: THE BOTTOM LINE

Once your fiancé slips the wedding ring on your finger, you'll know intellectually that you've just become his wife, but the psychological significance of your getting married may not hit you immediately or in ways you could have imagined, from the friends you keep to how you approach your job. In fact, most brides-to-be don't expect the huge psychological shift that they're bound to go through as they get used to the concept of who they are as married persons. In this chapter I suggested exercises you and your fiancé can do together to get comfortable with the concept of being married and to define the roles each of you will play in your married life (to simply assume he'll take out the garbage and you'll do the dishes without discussing these issues first is foolish), and discussed what friendships you'll continue, make anew, or let go of as you go from engaged to Mr. and Mrs.

A big decision for many brides involves last names—do you take his, keep yours, hyphenate, or create an entirely new name that you'll both start using? The whole name-change issue can end up causing more emotional upset than the wedding itself. Regardless of what you decide to do with your name, though, realize that it's a hard decision to make. Be sure to think of all the pros and cons of each name scenario before deciding and give yourself enough time to do so.

6

AVOIDING FAMILY FEUDS

AN AMAZING THING happens as you get into planning your wedding: family members and friends begin to reveal their true selves, and suddenly everyone has opinions about the decisions you're making (or not making) for your wedding. Your normally (or so you thought) mild-mannered mother overnight turns into a staunch advocate of Viennese tables as a must at the reception, and out of the blue your formerly and seemingly nonreligious grandparents start demanding that a highly Orthodox wedding ceremony is the only way to go. It's enough to make you want to pull out your hair—and perfect ammunition for the start of many family feuds.

Licensed psychotherapist, relationship expert, and author of *The Unofficial Guide to Dating Again* (Hungry Minds, 1999), Tina Tessina, Ph.D., likens the wedding-planning period to a microcosm of your life to come and an excellent window into the issues, temperaments, and demands you're likely to face again and again in your future life together. "This is all stuff you haven't dealt with before. For the first time, you're seeing people's true selves: they get stressed, and stuff just comes out," she says.

So what's a frazzled bride to do, when your fiancé's family is tugging you this way with their wants and demands and your family is tugging you that way with their expectations? Simple: start talking. Open the lines of communications. Get together for a tête-à-tête. Have a gestalt session. Go out for a couple of beers. Whatever you call it, the important thing is to start communicating with these people in your life. Otherwise, resentment will just build up, and you'll end up with something along the lines of "the Hatfields and McCoys plan a wedding but almost kill each other in the process." "If you establish good communication now and set boundaries with your friends and family, then what happens is you set a good pattern of how things are going to be for the rest of your married life," says Dr. Tessina. "If you establish this pattern now, you won't have to work as hard on communication issues later on."

KEYS TO COMMUNICATION

I realize that, for many families, the idea of communicating openly feels unnatural, but think about it this way: everyone communicates in his or her own way. Although you may like to talk things out until you feel spent, your father may communicate not with words but with subtle body language or by how often he calls you on the phone. So although I suggest that you keep those lines of communication open with your family, I don't expect that overnight you'll change your family's dynamics. Rather, I want you to become a keen observer of people's behavior, and then use that to your advantage to get what *you* want: a stress-free wedding.

For example, you may discover that when your future mother-in-law is confronted about her feelings, emotions, or opinions, she clams up. If she's secretly upset about certain choices you're making about your wedding—you know, because she's either hinted at them through other family members or she becomes icy cold whenever the topic of your wedding comes up—you've got to take the upper hand in the situation. Dr. Tessina suggests the following tact:

First, if the person in question is on your fiancé's side of the family, such as his mother, go to him first to get a lay of the land, if you will. "He's the expert who has known his mother his whole life, so find out what approach he thinks will work best with his mother," Dr. Tessina suggests. He may tell you that when it comes to tough topics, his mother prefers written communication, a phone conversation, or a mealtime discussion. Whatever he suggests, give it a go: write that E-mail, make that call, or invite your future mother-in-law out for lunch. Be up front about why you're getting in touch. Tell her you have the feeling that she's displeased with certain decisions that you're making about your wedding, so you've reached out to her to give her the chance to express her feelings. See what happens. If she starts denying that she's upset or stays silent, don't get frustrated.

The Lighter Side: Family Feuds

While I'd hate to see your family feuding over your wedding, you might enjoy a fun, lighthearted diversion to a website devoted entirely to the television game show "Family Feud." At familyfeud.tv you can read up on the show's history—the original "Family Feud," hosted by Richard Dawson, debuted in 1977—or play the game online.

Instead, say something like, "I'll assume that your silence or lack of opinion means that you're OK with whatever decision I make on the seating arrangements and the receiving line. As a courtesy to you, I'm letting you know how I'm handling these issues. If you don't like what I'm doing, please call or E-mail me next week so we can talk about it. I'm leaving it up to you to say something. Otherwise, I'm going through with my original plans." By setting the situation up this way, you've let your future mother-in-law know that her thoughts and opinions are important to you, but the fact that she refuses to express them is her problem, not yours. You've put the onus on her, and this way you're not waiting around for her to figure out how to communicate with you. If she ends up not saying anything, then you know you've done the right thing and you can move on. And she'll just have to learn to live with your decisions—and learn that she'd better speak up the next time she wants you to consider doing things her way.

One additional thought: if you know from past experience (or your fiancé has told you) that his mother (or whoever it is you're having trouble communicating with) is a perpetual procrastinator, then

---

Wedding Wisdom

From watching friends who have gone through horrible experiences with fights with their parents and their parents-to-be, I learned that the first thing you have to do is sit down all the parties at the beginning of the planning and come to an understanding about who will contribute to which part of the wedding—if at all. From these conversations with my parents and my fiancé's parents, we were able to create a realistic budget. And because the key to being open and honest with everyone is communicating, we nipped any problems in the bud.

BONNIE, ILLINOIS

set up the previously mentioned scenario with a firm deadline. Say something like, "If I don't hear from you by next Friday, this is what I'm going to do." If she happens to call you on Sunday with her suggestions, be firm. Remind her of the Friday deadline, and let her know that you're not going to change what you're doing just because she called *near* the deadline. Sure, the easy thing to do would be to say to yourself, "Oh, it's only two days later than what I'd asked for," but giving in now will likely set a precedent for future situations. You'll have shown this person that, under the gun, you're a pushover, and if she just waits until you're really stressed out about something to voice her opinions, she's likely to get her way.

Perhaps in reading this, you're saying, "But what about my fiancé? Why can't he handle everything having to do with his mother?" Well, that's a reasonable response, and you can rally his support in certain situations. But take a minute to think about the future: do you want to have to rely on your husband to intervene every single time someone in his family does something that upsets you? If you do, then you'll find yourself feeling paralyzed more than empowered, and frankly, it's not a healthy way to develop a relationship with your in-laws—or your fiancé with your family. By marrying this person, you're joining his family and he's joining yours, and you should grow comfortable with the idea of being able to communicate openly with each other's side of the family.

Now back to the problem at hand: an incommunicative family member, who is probably secretly harboring opinions about your wedding but isn't sharing them. You've tried the direct approach, and that doesn't seem to get you anywhere. Now you have two options: you can live with the fact that you tried to get your future mother-in-law (or whomever) to open up, and because she didn't, you're moving on to plan B, which is doing what you want anyway. Or, you can suggest that your fiancé attempt to handle things with his mother, but I don't think this is a good idea. As I mentioned earlier, this will establish a pattern of behavior with his parents that will leave you feeling helpless in the future. If you show them that when times get tough, you're going to wimp out and send their son to fix things, then they probably won't take you seriously whenever you attempt to open a dialogue with them—even if it's on something as mundane as planning a vacation to visit them. They'll be thinking, "Oh, isn't it sweet that Sue called us, but we know that they won't make any firm decisions until John calls us, so we'll just wait until then." Is this how you want your in-laws thinking of you? I think not.

"That's why a wedding is such a perfect microcosm of life," says Dr. Tessina. Whatever patterns you observe in getting ready for your wedding will be the patterns you'll see throughout your life. That's because people work in certain ways when they're in certain situations, and it's up to you to figure out how best to work within those patterns.

Now, mind you, not all of these models spell trouble. For example, if your future mother-in-law has been really helpful now with all of your wedding plans, that's great, because she'll probably be really helpful when—and if—the kids come along. However, if your father is overbearing (and always has been), and you're fighting with him about everything having to do with your wedding, that's how he'll be with everything you ever try to plan or do in the future, including raising your children. "If you do this well and get all these lines of communication established now," adds Dr. Tessina, "you'll have an easier time in the future."

STICKY SITUATIONS

Although planning a wedding is ripe with conflict possibilities, certain issues tend to be universal irritants that come up again and again as trouble spots in many weddings. In this section, I've identified four common sticky situations and then offered easy-to-follow solutions.

Sticky Situation 1: Money

Money causes some of the greatest conflicts in life, and a wedding is no exception. These money issues might range from how much to spend on the wedding to who's contributing what to the wedding fund to how much a wedding dress costs. In fact, money will be one of the first topics you'll deal with as you craft your guest list and look for a ceremony and reception space to accommodate your wedding. For example, if you discover that you've put together a 500-person guest list, but the only places that can hold a party of that size are way beyond your budget, you'll either have to cut your guest list or come up with an alternate plan for paying for your wedding. (More on guest list conflict later.) Let's go with the latter scenario—figuring out a better way to pay for your wedding.

There are a number of ways you can do it, all of which will involve financial considerations and compromise on both of your parts. Consider the following scenarios and then weigh the pros and cons of each:

> **Wedding Wisdom**
> *I found out that my fiancé's parents wanted to give my parents money to help pay for the wedding, but I knew my parents would never accept such a "gift." So his parents came up with a creative solution. They knew we preferred a band but our budget would only allow for a deejay, so they decided to give us a gift of the band for our reception.*
> KARA, OREGON

- You can cut down on your spending and increase your savings, which can cause conflict if one of you is a spender and doesn't want to give up lunches out or the gym membership to save for the wedding.

Wedding Wisdom

Finances were the main source of argument for us in the beginning. We both finally got tired of fighting and sat down to work out a solution. We did this by making a list of what we want to spend money on and then creating a budget. The key was compromise—I thought his spending so much money on golf seemed a little silly, while he could not understand why I needed money to buy new clothes each month. But, by working together and trying to see it from each other's point of view, we were able to develop a budget and work together to achieve our financial goals.

SARAH, ILLINOIS

• One or both of you can take better jobs with higher salaries, which will increase the money coming in, but it could cut down on your time together based on the job's demands. So, you need to ask yourself if you're prepared to make a financial change for a social sacrifice.

• You could each move to cheaper places to live—or move in together to save on rent, but that may not fit with your values and ideals on premarital cohabitation.

• If one or both of you owns a home, you could take out a home-equity line of credit or a loan. However, you need to determine if you would be willing to be saddled with such a large debt load before your wedding.

• You can ask your parents for financial help. I offer this last scenario because, even in this day and age of older brides and grooms who foot the wedding bill themselves, there are plenty of parents who are willing to help their children pay for their weddings—and have been planning for it for many years. If your parents fall into this category, that's great, but your work isn't done yet.

Finding Solutions

Early on in the wedding-planning period, you need to sit down with whoever is going to contribute to the wedding and have a very businesslike meeting. During this meeting (which can occur face-to-face or over the phone if parents live far away), you need to establish guidelines for your wedding and boundaries for suggestions. Lay out what you expect the wedding will cost, and then talk about how much (or little) input you'd like or will allow the contributors to have. For example, if the bride's parents are paying for the wedding cere-

---

Wedding Wisdom

My fiancé and I were engaged in February, and we acted quickly to begin saving for the wedding, the majority of which we paid for ourselves. Within a month, I broke the lease on my apartment and we rented a truck and moved my belongings into his townhouse. We laid out a plan: he would pay for housing, entertainment, and other necessary living expenses, and we would put my entire salary into the savings account. No ifs, ands, or buts. We made being frugal a lot of fun by trying new recipes at home, looking for good bottles of wine on sale, and going to reduced-price matinees or borrowing videos from the library. We managed to save $35,000 by the time of the wedding and with only 60 guests, we had money to spare, which we used toward the purchase of a new home and a no-expenses-spared honeymoon in San Francisco and the Napa Valley.

KAREN, MARYLAND

mony and reception, they may assume that they are going to have a say in the selection of each site, plus the menu for the reception. If you and your fiancé are OK with this, let them know up front. If you're not, you have to say so up front, as well. Of course, then you risk upsetting your parents. It's not unreasonable for them to feel that they have a right to offer opinions on something they're paying for.

Now you may find yourself back at square one: do you want to give in on certain aspects of your wedding so you can have a bigger, more expensive affair? Or would you prefer to have total control and therefore need to scale back your expectations? Ideally, a parent "is going to stand up and say, 'No problem, we'll pay for all this stuff, and you can do as you please,'" says Dr. Tessina, but that doesn't always happen. I hate to be sexist, but it's true: mothers sometimes live vicariously through their sons and daughters and hope to plan the weddings they never had. So often when money is involved, there is a hidden agenda. Likewise, parents who are professional businesspeople may see your wedding as just another business venture and therefore bring certain expectations to the whole thing. This is where those lines of communication come into play. You need to talk about all of this from the very beginning, and hopefully, by talking, you'll be able to figure out how best to manage money as you plan your wedding.

Sticky Situation 2: Ceremony and Religious Issues

When people of differing religions marry, the wedding ceremony is usually a battleground: right away, you get into issues of whose religion is going to be represented how, plus dealing with how you're going to combine traditions and other elements into one wedding ceremony. But even those who have the same or similar religious backgrounds can run into conflict. For example, two Catholics marrying may have very different views on the role the Catholic Church will play in their lives, including at their wedding. Both may want to be married in a Catholic church and have agreed on the ceremony location, but only one wants a full mass, or the family of the more religious of the two people expects that this will occur at the wedding.

Finding Solutions

Because religion can be such a sensitive topic, you need to talk up front about your expectation of your wedding ceremony. If one of you wants to be married by a member of the clergy and the other doesn't care either way, then I'd suggest going with the clergy option because it's more important to one of you. If the other person just says "I don't care" because it seems like the easy way out, that's no way to deal with such sensitive issues, and you need to start talking about why this person wants to avoid conflict. Maybe this person's parents forced him to attend church each weekend, and over time he learned that not fighting about going to church was the easiest way to deal with anything having to do with religion. When it comes to your wedding, though, each party should feel as if he or she has had a fair say in any decision-making process, so encourage your apathetic partner to speak up. You may discover that he has some strong feelings about the presence of clergy at the wedding, and perhaps you're willing to compromise on your wedding officiant because you realize that his not wanting clergy there is stronger than your desire to have clergy officiate. As with anything in your relationship, you have to communicate your wants and wishes and figure out a way to come to a compromise without anyone feeling as if he or she has gotten the short end of the stick. (For more on issues of religion and how they may affect the ceremony you plan, turn to Chapter 11, "Making Your Ceremony Matter.")

On another note, you may have a very clear vision of how you want your ceremony to run, and you know for certain that it will differ greatly from what either of your parents expect. For example, you both come from very traditional families, but you're planning an untraditional wedding ceremony. Again, communication is key. Sit them down, and tell them ahead of time what you're planning to do. Let them know right away how important this kind of wedding is to you, and because you thought that it might upset them to see such a twist on tradition that you wanted to make them aware of your choice ahead of time. Acknowledge that it's OK for them to be taken aback, and don't expect everyone to endorse your version of your wedding ceremony at first. By giving them fair warning about it, you're also giving them time to digest this information, and, ideally, over time, they'll come around to support your decision. Here's how Ralph and Ginger handled telling their families about their offbeat ceremony plans.

"We knew we would encounter the biggest amount of resistance from Ralph's family, so a few months before the wedding, we sat them down and just said straight out, 'Look, this wedding isn't going to be what you are expecting, and it might look kind of weird to you,'" Ginger recalls. "We went on to explain that we wanted our wedding ceremony to reflect who we are—fun, upbeat people. The last thing we wanted was for the ceremony to be this solemn affair, with everyone sitting there with their hands folded neatly in their laps. In addition, because so many of our friends and family members were pitching in to help with the wedding—my sister made my dress, a friend baked the cake, etc.—we wanted to have a chance to greet them before the wedding."

Adds Ralph, "When I heard Ginger's talk about wanting to greet people and shake their hands as she was walking down the aisle, I thought, 'Hey, I want to do that, too. I don't just want to be standing at the altar waiting for her.' So I told my parents that I would be coming into the church first and walking down the aisle."

Ralph and Ginger also let their parents know that their ceremony music of choice was a gospel choir, which would involve standing, singing, and clapping—and which was a severe departure from the Lutheran church atmosphere both had been raised in.

Even though they forewarned Ralph's parents of their ceremony choice, Ralph and Ginger still sensed some hesitancy on his parents' part, so they asked straight out, "Well, what's your problem with our choices?"

"And you know what was bugging them the most?" Ginger recalls. "They were afraid that their friends would be upset. So we asked them what we could do to help make them feel more comfortable, and all they wanted was permission to tell their friends in advance about the ceremony. They thought that we were going to swear them to secrecy or something, which was the farthest thing from our minds. We told them it was OK to talk to their friends, and things went so much more smoothly with his parents from that day forward."

Sticky Situation 3: Children at the Wedding

If your dream wedding has always involved petite flower girls with flowing hair and pretty dresses, but the last thing that you want to hear during your ceremony is a crying baby, then you're going to need to figure out how you're going to handle the issue of children at your wedding—because it's almost impossible to have one (the adorable flower girls) without the other (other people's young children). That is, if you decide that you absolutely must have your sister's children participating in your wedding ceremony, then you're going to have to do one of two things.

Finding Solutions

One, you must invite all children to your wedding and be willing to foot the bill to have someone watch or entertain them. For example, we hired a clown to keep the children at our wedding occupied. At another wedding to which our children were invited, the bride and groom had arranged to have a handful of baby-sitters available at the reception so the parents could enjoy themselves without having to chase after their toddlers all night long. (However, children were invited to and welcomed at the church ceremony.)

Two, you exclude children, except for those who will be participating in the wedding. If you go with this option, then the polite thing to do is to call each of your friends and family members with children and explain to them that although your sister Karen's children will be in the wedding—and will be handed off to a baby-sitter immediately after the ceremony—you are unable to include their children in the service or reception as well. For those who may not be 100 percent clear about what you're saying or who may feign indifference because they intend to bring their children anyway, you may want to put your subtlety on the shelf and say something stronger, for instance, "This is an adults-only wedding. Unfortunately, your children are not welcome."

If you don't want to deal with the hassle of either scenario, then you must scale back your expectations for young people to be a part of your wedding ceremony, and don't include any children. Sure, some people will be unhappy with whatever child-related decision you make, but they'll just have to get over it.

Sticky Situation 4: Passive Groom

I don't mean to slam your fiancé, but I know how men can get when they're planning a wedding. As soon as you starting querying them on their preferences and opinions, you get something like, "Whatever you want, dear, is fine with me" or "Just tell me what kind of tux to get and when I have to show up, and I'll be sure to be there." I think most men recognize that we women plan out our dream weddings starting in childhood, and chances are we have a pretty clear idea in our heads of what we want for our wedding. But what you've got to make clear to your fiancé is this: although that assessment may be true, he needs to understand that this is *your* wedding together, and as much as you want your dreams to come true, you want this wedding to be about what *he* wants as well.

Finding Solutions

Sometimes men adopt a passive nature in wedding plans because they grew up in a household where there was a strict division of labor: Dad mowed the lawn and took care of certain things around the house; social events, like giving a dinner party or, dare we say, planning a wedding, was Mom's job. And never the twain shall meet: Dad knew that he shouldn't offer his opinions about social plans because Mom wouldn't hear any of it, and Mom wouldn't comment on the landscaping because that was Dad's territory. Your fiancé may have unconsciously lumped you in with his mother. That means he isn't offering any wedding suggestions because, based on his parents' roles, there were never any compromises to be had between husband and wife. Well, you can't let this all play out again in your own marriage.

You need to let your fiancé know that you want to hear what he has to say and that together you'll figure out a way to make this wedding what you both want. Besides, "if your fiancé resents the whole wedding thing, hates every minutes of it, and feels like what he wanted didn't count, that sets up a bad dynamic for the couple," warns Dr. Tessina, "including the possibility of unconscious payback." No one wants to go into a new marriage with one person feeling slighted, so talk it out.

GETTING YOUR PARENTS INVOLVED

Sometimes, the best defense against wedding-planning sticky situations and future family feuds is a good offense. In this instance, that means involving the parents up front. Start by giving each parent a chance to say his or her piece. Find out what their fantasies of their children's weddings are and hear them out. This will benefit all of you in three ways. One, it will give the parents a chance to feel as if they've had their say. Two, it will make them realize you care enough about them to ask for their thoughts and opinions. And, three, it will give you the opportunity to hear what your parents' hopes and dreams are, and you can see if they somehow match up with your vision for your wedding. If they do, perhaps you can adopt some of their suggestions, which will be a big ego boost for them and make you feel good in that you somehow pleased your parents. After all, that's what most kids want to do, so if you can do so without compromising your own values, great!

Another great way to get your parents involved—and make them feel wanted—is to take advantage of any special skills they may possess. If your father is a music teacher, ask him to come with you as you interview deejays and bands for the reception. If your mother-in-law is an accomplished

> **Wedding Wisdom**
> Because it was too stressful trying to plan a wedding with "everyone's hands in the pot"—meaning our families' influence—we decided to move forward with planning the wedding without our families' help (emotionally or monetarily). It has made the planning a thousand times easier.
> TEREZ, NEW YORK

seamstress—and you're into the idea of a custom-made wedding gown—see if she would consider making your dress.

Finally, if there are family traditions that your parents have suggested you use in your wedding, see if there isn't some way you can work them into your ceremony. I know it's important for your wedding to reflect who you are, and sometimes we as brides become controlling beasts, but when it comes to family traditions, doing a little something to make someone happy can go a long way toward creating goodwill. So, if your mother asks that you carry the same light blue handkerchief that she carried at her wedding—and that your grandmother and great-grandmother carried at their weddings before you—don't immediately dismiss the idea as sappy sentimentality. If this handkerchief is really important to your family tradition and it really won't kill you to tuck it into your garter belt or keep it in your purse, then do it. "These traditions really have to do with loss, and if you haven't lost grandparents yet, you won't understand how important it is to have a piece of your past with you at your wedding," says Dr. Tessina. "It really is critical to keep connections between people, and that's what family traditions accomplish: connections with the past."

DEALING WITH DIVORCED PARENTS

As the child of divorce, I can tell you that planning a wedding with divorced parents can be ten times as difficult as planning a wedding with parents who are still married. If divorced parents have remarried, there are twice as many individuals weighing in with opinions on your wedding and that many more personalities you have to deal with. But the one constant that you need to recognize up front and deal with immediately is the issue of behavior patterns.

If your parents have feuded from the day they signed the divorce papers and have made every birthday, graduation, and holiday a living nightmare, why should your wedding be any different? That's why you have to be the grown-up in the situation. Open the lines of communication early with your parents and lay out in no uncertain terms exactly how you expect them to behave at your wedding. By doing so, you may be able to avoid conflict altogether.

"You need to sit them down and say, 'Look, you are going to get along for this occasion, whatever it takes,'" Dr. Tessina advises. "'I will not have you arguing at this wedding like you do at every family get-together. And if you don't think you can do that, then I don't want you at my wedding.'"

Wedding Wisdom

I took extra special care in the seating arrangements, so my divorced parents would both feel comfortable. My father is remarried and my mother isn't, so I was particularly careful with her feelings. I sat them at different tables during the reception, and I even gave the tables cute names instead of numbers, to avoid having to seat anyone at the number one table.

SARA, NEW YORK

Yes, making this kind of ultimatum is difficult, but it is necessary. Now, if your parents agree to get along at the wedding—even if that means giving each other the silent treatment—then you need to do your part, too, in making them as comfortable as possible. Seat them in separate ends of the same aisle at the ceremony, put them at tables on the opposite side of the dance floor at the reception, and don't expect that they'll stand together in the receiving line. During this conversation, let them know of your desire to help make the affair as easy to get through as possible for all involved, but be clear that you also expect that the parents won't bad-mouth each other to guests and, should they find themselves in line together at the buffet table, that they'll be polite and put on a good face.

In addition, look to your extended family for support. For example, designate an aunt or cousin to be the guardian of your parents at the wedding. That way, should your mom dissolve into tears when your dad arrives with his new wife or your father-in-law starts drinking too much and making off-color jokes about his ex-wife (your future mother-in-law), this guardian can whisk the upset or offending party away to the restrooms or the lobby and far from other guests.

Or, if the whole idea of confronting your parents about their behavior at your wedding terrifies you, turn to your fiancé for support. Put your heads together to figure out a game plan for talking with the feuding parents. "Doing so is a really good exercise for marriage—for when you and your husband need to strategize how you'll handle a difficult situation," says Dr. Tessina. Your fiancé may sug-

Wedding Wisdom

My parents are divorced and not friendly, so one of the first things I decided after we got engaged was that I wasn't going to let money become an issue, as it was with my parents' divorce. I laid down the law from the start. My fiancé and I told all of our parents that we were going to plan the wedding ourselves, and the parents could help if they wanted. That is, anyone could give us a gift of money, but they couldn't say what it was to be used for and no one was allowed to pay for particular things (e.g., the cake, the bar bill, the rehearsal dinner). Granted, we needed and expected help as we couldn't afford to pay for the whole wedding on our own, but this was the only way to make sure we kept my parents from fighting or anyone from "owning" a particular part of the wedding. And you know what? It worked!

SARA, NEW YORK

gest being with you when you have this conversation with your parents so that if you get stymied or start to chicken out, he can jump in and help you finish the task.

Sometimes, professional help is called for. "If there are so many leftover and unresolved feelings from the divorce, then therapy is a good idea," says Dr. Tessina. You can go it alone, or you can ask your mother or father or both parents to join you.

BALANCE: THE BOTTOM LINE

No couple wants to have their families end up like the Hatfields and McCoys, but unless you open the lines of communications early in the engagement period, you and your fiancé's family may end up that way. In this chapter I've identified the four most common sticky situations that lead to family feuds—money, religion, children at the wedding, and a passive groom—and the solutions for avoiding them.

I've also offered a no-doubt defensive strategy when dealing with parents—divorced or not—and that's a good offense. Recognize the trouble spots ahead of time and offer concrete solutions to your parents. By putting your foot down and being the grown-up in this situation, you can guarantee that your wedding plans will involve fewer fights—if not none at all—than most do. That's exactly how it should be.

7

Don't Forget Yourself

It's amazing what happens to a woman when she gets engaged. First, she accepts her beloved's proposal of marriage. Then, almost immediately, she has a to-do list that's ten pages long and growing. Suddenly, she's gone from wondering when her boyfriend will pop the question to wondering how she will ever get everything done before her wedding. There are reception sites to visit, menus to sample, photographers to interview, dresses to try on, musicians to listen to, and more. In fact, even as you read this book, you may be scribbling notes in the margins about what you need to do next.

Well, I say, stop for a moment. Close your eyes, take a deep breath, and then exhale it slowly. Did it? OK, do it again. Great. Now, do it one more time. Do you feel better? I'm sure you do, even if it's just a little bit.

You may be wondering why I just suggested you stop reading to take some deep breaths. It's because I, too, was once a bride, and I know how hectic planning a wedding can be. If you don't remind yourself to stop every once in a while and take care of yourself during this very busy period, you're going to end up stressed out and exhausted on your wedding day—if not before. Plus, studies have shown that as little as five minutes a day of stress management, such as by doing deep-breathing exercises, can significantly improve your overall health. That's why along with all your wedding-related appointments, I want you to schedule time for *you*!

As I mentioned in the book's introduction, it's all too common for a bride-to-be to catch what I call "I Do Disease." That is, her wedding becomes an all-consuming matter in her life, and she puts taking care of herself on the back burner—*way* on the back burner. For instance, since you became engaged, when was the last time you allowed yourself the "luxury" of going to bed early? Put aside thirty minutes to take a walk or ride your bike? Ate a healthy meal, during which you weren't reading bridal magazines, talking on the phone, scribbling notes to yourself, or surfing wedding websites? Putting yourself second in the grand scheme of things is a really bad idea. That's because when you don't take care of yourself, you're just not going to function as well on a day-to-day basis. In addition, you won't look as good if you're stressed out or lacking sleep. That's why you've got to make stress management and relaxation as much a part of your wedding plans as finding the perfect dress.

Think of it this way: putting together a wedding is like putting together a giant business conference. We wouldn't think it was a good idea for someone who was responsible for an important corporate event to go without sleep or without taking a break, because we know that person wouldn't function well. Why should a bride (or groom, for that matter) be any different?

One bride I know immediately recognized the importance of taking care of herself. Her name is Roseanne, and she's a publicist in New York City. If you follow her lead, you, too, can arrive at the altar a calmer, healthier, more beautiful bride. Let me tell you about how Roseanne became a balanced bride.

LOOKING ROSY

Because part of what Roseanne does as a publicist is plan events for her clients, she accepted that planning her own wedding was going to be a huge undertaking. Soon after she became engaged—and with her wedding a little more than a year away—Roseanne scheduled pampering sessions for herself for the next twelve months. It was time just for her, away from the stress of her wedding. Most importantly, it gave Roseanne time to relax, reflect, and rejuvenate.

Starting a year in advance of her wedding, Roseanne began getting her eyebrows waxed. This was the first time she'd ever had this service done. "I didn't want my eyebrows to be these bushy, unmanageable things above my eyes when I got married," she says. "I knew that if I got them in shape now—and then maintained them over that year—they would look fantastic on my wedding day."

Then, about six months before the wedding, Roseanne started going for biweekly manicures. She stepped up the manicure pace three months later and began having manicures weekly. This helped Roseanne in a number of ways. "I often bite or chew on my nails when I get stressed, and my life was very stressful then," she says. "I was working eleven- to fourteen-hour days, planning for my wedding, and dealing with all sorts of family situations." However, because she was taking the time to manicure her nails—and they always looked so good—Roseanne was able to kick the nail-biting habit, despite her stress level. This left her hands and nails looking beautiful for all of her wedding-related events, like her bridal shower, and for the big day as well.

About four months before her wedding, Roseanne began having facials every three weeks. "I added in hour-long massages several times when I scheduled my facial appointments," she says. Makeup artists she interviewed for the big day were constantly complimenting her on the fabulous shape of her eyebrows and the superior state of her skin.

Then, a few days before the big day, Roseanne stopped working. This extra time before her wedding allowed for additional pampering. One day, she had a marathon session at a day spa. Her treatments included a massage, body scrub, and facial. "It was the perfect excuse to take time and chill out," she says. "The whole time I was at the spa I wasn't looking at my watch, my cell phone was off, and I was completely relaxed."

Roseanne's mind, body, and spirit (not to mention her nails, skin, and eyebrows) were in tip-top shape the day she walked down the aisle. She's extremely thankful that she invested her time in pampering herself before her wedding. "I finally understand why some women—especially some of the female executives you read about in magazines—spend tons of money on facials, massages, and the like," she adds. "After all the stress of my wedding and constantly being on the go, those luxuries were a great way to force me to take a time-out. Devoting several hours a month to yourself is not that much when you look at the bigger picture of the crazy,

---

Wedding Wisdom

I made a point of going for facials once a month for the eight months prior to my wedding. I'd had facials before, but they'd always been a luxury. This time they were a necessity. They worked and really cleared up my skin up. I wanted to look the most beautiful that I could on my wedding day, and these regular facials helped me feel better about myself overall.

MELISSA, PENNSYLVANIA

hectic lives we lead—especially when you throw planning a wedding into the mix."

She continues: "To meet the needs of everyone in their families, brides sometimes forget to meet *their* needs. For me, these services helped me take time out and concentrate on myself."

MENTAL-HEALTH BOOST

I couldn't have said it better myself. What Roseanne's story exemplifies is that when you take time to take care of yourself, you're doing your body and your mind a world of good. There's actually a real psychological benefit derived from taking time for yourself: your brain gets the time it needs to sort through everything that has been going on in your life lately. Without this mental break, your brain can't function as efficiently, and you can't think clearly. In essence, downtime gives your mental health a much-needed boost—and you a better outlook on life. This improved outlook will prepare you for any curveballs you encounter as you plan your wedding.

It did with Roseanne, who found herself able to deal with wedding snafus in a calmer, more clearheaded way. For example, when her wedding dress arrived two sizes too small (because the dress shop hadn't measured her properly) and then her florist went out of business just thirty days before the wedding, Roseanne didn't freak out. Instead, she credits her regularly scheduled pampering sessions, which allowed her to "forget about all my problems planning for the wedding," with granting her

> **Wedding Wisdom**
> *The main thing I did was plan my life around exercising instead of the other way around. No matter what was going on, I would plan to work out from 5:00–6:00 or 6:30, which wasn't too hard to do once I got into the habit.*
>
> JENNY, NEW YORK

the resolve to find solutions to both the dress and florist problems without giving herself an ulcer.

Here's another benefit to pampering yourself: certain spa treatments, such as a deep-tissue massage, relax your entire body in such a way that you'll get a better night's sleep. And we all know how a good night's sleep can do wonders for improving our attitude the next morning.

But taking time for yourself doesn't always have to be an expensive trip to the spa. Going for a walk during your lunch hour or allowing yourself to soak in the tub once a week can leave you feeling happy and serene, just like a massage might. Or you can schedule time every Friday night, for example, to give yourself a manicure and pedicure at home. It will give you time away from planning your wedding, and you'll come away relaxed *and* with great-looking nails!

Don't forget that doing exercise counts as time for yourself as well. One bride-to-be in Kansas started taking a karate class soon after she became engaged. Her three-times-a-week class was a great way for her to stop obsessing about her wedding and start focusing on herself. Plus, working with the punching bag did wonders for stress relief and gave her awesome-looking arms for the sleeveless sheath wedding dress she was planning to wear. Another engaged woman in Massachusetts made sure that she continued her morning swims, even though she was tempted to cancel them to accomplish more on her wedding to-do list. If you prefer to do your exercise at home or can't afford a gym membership, try borrowing a yoga videotape (or a video of any other kind of exercise you prefer) from your local library and using it two to three times a week as part of your self-care routine.

Wedding Wisdom

I've been a runner for years, but during the months before the wedding I found that I needed my runs more than ever for stress relief.

KELLY, ILLINOIS

COUPLE TIME

If you're not convinced yet that you need to take time for you, consider this: not only does giving yourself a time-out away from your wedding plans do wonders for your mental health, but it can also help your relationship with your fiancé. Here's a thought: why not give each other an engagement gift of a couple's massage? That way you'll both have time to relax, and you'll be able to spend some quality time together.

Jim Leemon, owner of a holistic day spa in Philadelphia, says couples who get pampered together communicate better. At Leemon's spa, called Terme di Aroma, customers are encouraged to hang out in their bathrobes in the spa's lounge, relaxing on the comfy couches, enjoying a complimentary cup of herbal tea or wine, and talking among themselves for as long as they like. For engaged couples, this soothing environment can have an amazing effect. Leemon, who's also a licensed therapist, says he's seen many couples work out wedding problems during this relaxing, postpampering time.

"For the first time in a long time, the couple are in a place where they're relaxed," he says. "The stress is off, they're sitting in robes, and they open up a little more to each other."

You can re-create this kind of soothing environment by booking time at a spa for both of you, or you can attempt to achieve this effect at home for free. Here's how:

One weekend morning, why don't you each take a long soak in the tub—together, if you can fit and if it fits your lifestyle. Then, put on what I like to call "comfy clothes" (sweats, pajamas, or anything loose and comfortable) and just hang out together. Turn the telephone ringer off. Don't turn on the television. Just be in the same room with each other and see what happens. You may feel weird at first, just sitting there and staring at each other. But give it some time. I bet that you'll find yourself starting to talk—and talk about things in a way that you haven't been able to for weeks, if not months. Try to give yourselves an hour of this "together time" each week, and I'm sure you'll come away feeling a lot more relaxed and a lot closer than you did the day before.

Another option is to have your fiancé give you a massage to get rid of the knots in your shoulders and back—and you can do the same for him. Try to help each other relax on a regular basis, and not only will the two of you get one-on-one time, but you'll also receive some free stress relief.

THE SPA EXPERIENCE

Even though I'm sure you have a million things to do as you plan your wedding, not knowing where to go to get pampered or how to give yourself a manicure can't be your excuse for neglecting yourself. Here are some suggestions on finding great spas and salons near where you live or work, tips on getting to the spa on time, and ideas on keeping the spa experience affordable:

- Call SpaFinders, a New York–based company that acts as a clearinghouse of spa information nationwide. Call 800-ALL-SPAS.
- Look in local magazines (either print or on the Web) for advertisements or articles on local spas.
- Check out magazines that are heavy on beauty, like *Allure* and *InStyle*. For example, each month *Allure*'s "Directory" section and *InStyle*'s "Black Book" column highlight spas and salons around the country that specialize in different

kinds of services at a variety of price levels. Visit your local library to read up on back issues.
- Ask your friends, family, or colleagues where they go to get pampered.

Once you find a spa or salon you want to visit—or even if you decide that you're going to do your beauty services yourself—make sure taking care of yourself becomes a priority. A good way to ensure you won't end up missing a spa appointment or blowing off your at-home facial is to schedule it in advance, and enter the appointment in your calendar (yes, even if you're doing it at home). Ask the spa or salon to call you the day before your appointment as a reminder. Or, if you're doing the beauty routine yourself, enlist your maid of honor to be your conscience (and reminder service). Have her call or E-mail you the day before your planned pampering so you don't end up neglecting yourself.

> **Wedding Wisdom**
> *I made regular appointments at the local day spa for facials, pedicures, and massages, as well as a few body wraps. You only get married once, and I wanted to make the best of it!*
> JANE, MASSACHUSETTS

Here's another idea: try to schedule a series of appointments in advance. With all you have on your plate, it's easy to say that you're going to get a weekly manicure or monthly massage and then not follow through because you haven't already committed the time. But if everything is already scheduled ahead of time—and you receive a reminder call before each appointment—you'll find it harder to neglect yourself.

If you decide to go the spa and salon way, you will probably want to make the experience as affordable as possible. With that in mind, here are some ways to ensure that your self-care spending doesn't get out of control:

• When you schedule your appointments, don't be shy about asking if the spa offers a discount to customers who book a block of services at once. Some salons may have a "pay for eight, get ten manicures" deal, so ask if yours does anything similar.

• See if you can register at your favorite spa or salon for a variety of services. That way, engagement and bridal shower gifts can all be put toward your self-care series. Or, if you're not comfortable registering at a spa, or if the spa doesn't offer such a service, then you can tell anyone who asks about bridal gifts that you would enjoy a gift certificate from such-and-such spa or salon. These gift certificates are also a good idea for holidays and birthdays, and you can suggest them as such.

• Indulge in just one manicure, pedicure, facial, or body treatment before your wedding. Then, while you're at the spa and in the throes of a treatment, pick the technician's brain. Tell her that although you would love to get a weekly manicure or monthly facial, you sim-

---

Wedding Wisdom

I have always been a big fan of beauty treatments and products, but also have had a hard time justifying spending time and money on something like how I look. However, once I got engaged I decided to make a more concentrated effort to improve my appearance. I decided to build a "beauty fund" into my budget. I began getting bimonthly manicures to make sure my nails were in strong, healthy shape by the wedding, as well as regular appointments for bikini and eyebrow waxes.

SARAH, ILLINOIS

ply can't afford it. Let her know that you're interested in being able to do these things for yourself at home, and ask her to recommend products or ways of doing things so that you can re-create the experience at home. Most professionals in the beauty business are happy to share how-to information with their clients because they know that doing so builds goodwill and great relationships. For example, I love the way my hairstylist blows straight my naturally wavy hair. During a hair appointment last year, I told her that I had a few black-tie events coming up and that I would love to hire her to do my hair before each affair—that is, if I could afford the expense. She asked me how I was planning on wearing my hair, and when I answered "Blown straight," she insisted on giving me an impromptu (and free) lesson then and there on the best way to make my hair as silky soft as she does. The ten minutes she took during a regular haircut to teach me these skills were invaluable, and I'm still using them now whenever I need my hair to look perfect.

Remember: once you start pampering yourself on a regular basis and seeing how much better you look and feel, you're more likely to continue your self-care routine.

THE DO-IT-YOURSELF BRIDE

When your bathroom needed painting, did you do it yourself? When your best friend got married, did you make all the favors at her bridal shower by hand? Do you love watching Home and Garden Television? If you answered "yes" to any of these questions, you're probably a do-it-yourself (or DIY) bride. This DIY-ness, if you will, probably extends to self-care services, and I'll bet you're the kind of woman who would prefer to give herself a manicure rather than let a stranger do it. Or, perhaps your wedding budget simply won't allow extravagant indulgences at the spa. Either way, here is an easy way to create an at-home spa so you can reap the benefits of pampering without spending a lot of money.

The center of your at-home spa should be your bathroom, but before you draw a bath, take some time to change the scenery.

Bring a portable CD player into the bathroom and put on some soothing tunes. (My favorite is anything by Enya.) Then, light some candles (scented ones are nice), and turn off the overhead lights.

After you've gotten undressed and before you start to soak, step into the tub and give yourself an allover body scrub. This scrub will remove dead skin and leave your skin glowing. You can use a sea sponge or washcloth with a store-bought scrub. Just don't rub too hard. Use the shower to rinse off. Then, fill the tub, get in, and soak.

If you want to use aromatherapy products to enhance your mood, look for bath salts or oils with lavender, chamomile, or sandalwood. All are great scents for relaxing. Otherwise, just add plain old Epsom salts to your water. It works wonderfully to help soothe sore muscles.

Because you'll be soaking for about twenty minutes, you may want to treat other parts of your body as well. You can give your hair a deep-conditioning treatment or slather a moisturizing mask on your face.

Don't forget to take care of your feet and hands. After you've dried off and climbed into comfortable clothes, coat your hands and feet with a moisturizing cream. Then pull a pair of clean socks on your feet and another pair on your hands. (The socks will trap heat from your hands and feet and help the cream soak in.) Then go lie down for another ten or twenty minutes. If you want, use a folded hand towel to cover your eyes, and cover yourself with a blanket. This extra time will not only allow the foot and hand treatment to work, but it will also give you a few more minutes of downtime before you have to deal with the real world again.

Should you ever run low on ideas for your at-home spa treatments, head back to the library and check out back issues of women's magazines like *Redbook*, *Family Circle*, and *Ladies' Home Journal*, which will often give step-by-step instructions on certain beauty treatments. When you find an article you like, make a copy of it so you can try it at home.

If you don't have the time to collect a variety of products for your at-home spa, don't fret. Jaqua Girls, a hip California company, offers a $35 "Urban Survival Kit," which comes packaged in a paint can and is available at Bloomingdale's or through the Femail Creations catalog (femailcreations.com). It's packed with a ton of stuff to help you relax, including a CD of soothing music, a body massager, and aromatherapy products.

COUNTDOWN TO "I DO"

Here is a countdown calendar for all the beauty services you may want or need to have done in advance of your wedding. I've created this calendar so that it applies to all brides-to-be—those who have a year to plan for their wedding as well as those who have only a few months to go. In addition, I've suggested services that would be appropriate for a woman who doesn't have a pampering regimen in place (except for shaving her legs and getting a haircut every now and again) and a woman who has already gotten into the habit of getting her hair colored regularly or nails done on a weekly basis. In addition, you can follow this calendar at a spa or salon, or you can do many of these services yourself at home. Furthermore, feel free to choose only the service or services that suit you. What's important is that you're taking the time to take care of *you*.

Six Months Before the Wedding

• Start getting waxed, either by using a kit you buy in a drugstore or by paying for the service at a salon. Most women should focus on the legs and bikini area, especially if they're going to a tropical climate for their honeymoons and don't want the hassle of shaving. Also, consider getting your eyebrows waxed to avoid the ordeal of constant plucking. If you do, have this done professionally. I would hate to have you get overzealous with the wax and end up eyebrowless.

Some women also have unwanted hair on their upper lips, forearms, and backs—all of which can be waxed away. Getting the latter two areas waxed in advance of the wedding is key if you're going to be wearing a revealing dress and you don't like the way your forearms and back look with hair on them.

The benefit of waxing is twofold. One, hair doesn't grow back for six to eight weeks (although the two to three weeks you'll spend growing the hair to get it long enough for the wax to grip can be unpleasant). And, two, when it does grow back, it usually does so more sparsely. After your first waxing, you'll have to do a touch-up wax about every two months, but those touch-ups will likely be less intense than the first session—and go much faster!

> **Wedding Wisdom**
>
> *I have prescheduled regular hair and makeup appointments for the remaining months before my wedding so I don't slack off.*
>
> KARA, OREGON

Note: to make waxing less painful, keep the following in mind. Try to schedule your waxing appointments for *after* your period. You're more sensitive to pain when your hormones are raging during the premenstrual time. Also, when in doubt, take a dose of a pain reliever one hour before you get waxed so that it won't hurt as much.

• Begin getting or giving yourself a monthly facial. Because skin cells regenerate approximately every twenty-eight days, there's no reason to schedule facials more frequently than once a month. Keep in mind that getting regular facials is critical to your overall look (think wedding photographs). Your makeup will only be as beautiful as the skin it's applied to, and skin that has been treated to regular facials just glows.

• Go for a cut and color consultation with your stylist (or whoever will be doing your hair for your wedding). With twenty-four weeks to go before the walk down the aisle, you'll have plenty of time to experiment with different colors (should you choose to go that route), grow out a cut you don't like, or just let your hair get a little longer so you can wear an upswept hairdo at your wedding.

Three Months Before the Wedding

• Schedule weekly massages. With the clock ticking down to the big event, your stress level will probably accelerate. Now is the time to have a professional work out the kinks and knots that you're likely to have in your shoulders, back, or wherever it is that you accumulate your stress. If you can, try to schedule a couple's massage, which some spas now offer. They'll set up side-by-side massage tables for you and your fiancé, and massage therapists will work on you simul-

Massage

If one of the ways you decide to pamper yourself before your wedding is with a massage, I highly recommend that you find a spa that offers La Stone Therapy, or Hot Rocks massage. It's a unique method of massage whereby warm river stones, as well as the therapist's hands, are used to knead and relax muscles. La Stone is about more than just massage, though. Specially trained therapists who do La Stone turn what could be a ho-hum massage into an almost ritualistic experience, with Chinese gongs, lighted candles, and the sounds of falling water. The stones are supposed to help open up a person's energy fields. To that end, the therapist lays the stones along different energy meridians on the body and clicks stones over the client's body as well. This is definitely a New Age experience, but you'll be amazed at how well La Stone massage can bring relief to stressed-out muscles.

taneously. If a professional massage is too much for your budget, at least ask your fiancé to rub your shoulders once a week.

• Arrange for a weekly manicure (and biweekly pedicure). Again, you can pay a professional to do these services, or you can do them yourself. Whipping your cuticles into shape often takes more than one session at the manicurist's table. Plus, if you've never indulged in a manicure or pedicure, it may take some time for you to get used to the neat and trimmed look that comes from getting your nails done regularly, which is why you want to start these treatments now. If you're tempted to cancel, don't. Just remember that a diamond ring looks best on a well-manicured hand!

One to Two Months Before the Wedding

• Continue your facial, massage, manicure, pedicure, and waxing routine. You're almost down to the wire now, so it's imperative that you maintain your state of bliss and beauty that you've worked so hard to achieve.

• Interview and find someone to do your wedding-day hair and makeup, if you choose to have them done professionally. By allowing four to eight weeks for this search, you'll be sure to find someone whose personality meshes with yours and who knows exactly how to make you look beautiful for your big day.

• If you're going to do your makeup yourself, schedule an appointment for a makeover at a cosmetics counter in the department store or boutique where you buy your makeup. Be sure you bring a swatch of your dress so the makeup person can plan your makeup colors accordingly. Don't be afraid to have some fun by trying a new eye shadow or lip color.

One Week Before the Wedding

• Consider getting a body bronzing. If you'll be honeymooning in the tropics and want to give your skin color a little boost (without subjecting yourself to the dermatologist-despised tanning booths or the natural tanning rays of the sun), arrange to have a body bronzing done. Spas use high-end self-tanners, which are applied with a sponge paintbrush for an even-looking tan and which give your skin a sun-kissed glow that goes way beyond the orangey QT look of years ago. Plus, you don't have to worry about exposing your skin to any sun damage. This service is perfect if you don't want to look pale your first day at the beach or washed out in your wedding gown.

> ### Wedding Wisdom
> *I got a body bronzing at a salon. It was awesome, and I was tanner than ever in my life. White and ivory looked gorgeous against my newly bronzed skin.*
>
> SARA, NEW YORK

• Have a full-body polish. This is a mild exfoliation from shoulders to toes. An aesthetician will use a scrub applied to your skin with either her fingertips or a sea sponge to lightly polish away dead and flaking skin. (See "The Do-It-Yourself Bride" section of this chapter on how to do a body polish yourself.) It leaves the skin looking and feeling like silk. Note: if you're going to splurge for the body bronzing, do it *after* the body scrub. Otherwise, your fake tan will get scrubbed right off.

BALANCE: THE BOTTOM LINE

The easiest thing to do when faced with planning a wedding is to put taking care of yourself at the bottom of your to-do list, but this chapter has given you all the beauty reasons why you shouldn't do that. If you want to look fabulous on your wedding day, you've got to feel fabulous, and a big part of feeling fabulous is pampering yourself. I'm not saying that you have to spend thousands of dollars on a spa regime (although it would be nice if you can afford it, and I offered some suggested ways for finding great spas). Rather, what it really comes down to is this: do something nice for yourself on a regular basis. Take a long soak in the tub every Sunday morning. Go for a daily lunch-hour walk. Do your nails once a week. All of these little things will add up to your feeling a lot more relaxed and better about yourself on the big day.

To help you get your pampering routine on the right track, I've offered a "Countdown to 'I Do'" calendar so you can figure out when to add massage to the mix and at what point a pedicure might be nice. If you're at all in doubt about the benefits of a beauty routine, go back and reread the story of Roseanne, the balanced bride who put taking care of herself at the top of her list and ended up looking rosy and beautiful on her wedding day.

8

BALANCING WORK, FAMILY, AND FRIENDS

It MAY BE hard for the modern bride to believe, but not too long ago, the Internet was simply not a wedding-planning option. There was no Web to surf, E-mail to communicate with a bridal party, or chat rooms where you could compare wedding notes with other brides-to-be. As a currently plugged-in woman who primarily communicates with family via E-mail and gets the majority of her news and information off the Internet, even I have a hard time remembering what life was like before the virtual world came to be.

When I think back on my own wedding plans in the early 1990s, I realize how hard I had it—as did brides for years—in attempting to plan my wedding while working full time. For example, if I wanted to research vendors, read up on wedding-planning tips, or communicate with my wedding party, there were limited ways to do so—basically, I'd have to use the phone or meet them in person. Although that's still a reasonable way to do things, especially when hiring companies for your wedding, today you can visit a website and see streaming video of the band in action. (Of course, I recommend that you see the band live as well before booking them.) Having this option lets you narrow your choices without leaving the comfort of your home—or office, as the case may be. In addition, you can supplement the wedding books you buy with visits to the hundreds of websites that specialize in wedding-planning information. Finally, the ways of getting in touch with your wedding party vary across the board—from group E-mails and discussion groups to conference calls on cell phones.

PLAN YOUR WEDDING WITHOUT LOSING YOUR JOB

Sure, planning your wedding is still like taking on a full-time job when you already have one, but technology has made doing both well much easier. Here are some ways you can use technology, savvy strategies, and common sense to plan your wedding without infuriating your boss or losing your job and your mind.

> **Wedding Wisdom**
>
> *I used the Internet during lunch hours to do planning, as well as in the evenings when I got home from work. In fact, I got a DSL line at home so I could use the Internet more efficiently. I found great ideas and information on vendors online.*
>
> MELISSA, PENNSYLVANIA

Research Company E-Mail and Internet Availability

Now that you're engaged, you'll clearly be tempted to take advantage of your work Web connection to plan your wedding. Don't do it without knowing ahead of time what the ramifications of that action are. Find out first what your employer's policy on E-mail and Internet use is before you start surfing the Web for wedding information. It's no secret that employers are cracking down on personal use of company computers to do everything from sending a quick E-mail to Mom to holiday shopping online. Some have even secretly installed tracking software that will follow where and when each employee goes on the Internet and make secret copies of E-mails sent and received — even those that have been dragged and dropped into the desktop trash bin. So proceeding with caution is especially critical.

Talk to your human resources manager and see what the company's position is on personal use of computers during company time. You may discover that sending E-mails before eight in the morning, between the hours of twelve and two (typically lunchtime), or after five-thirty is acceptable. If so, plan your day accordingly and arrive early, eat lunch at your desk, or stay late, and use those approved times to do all of your wedding-related Web surfing. If not, do it all at home, either before you go to work or after you get home.

> ### Wedding Wisdom
>
> *I used the Internet to narrow my choices on all of the wedding planning — bridal registry, music options, band choices, flower design and selections, and transportation — and included my E-mail address for RSVPs. Using the Internet saved me lots of time and was very helpful during a busy time at work.*
>
> JUDY, NEW JERSEY

Explore Phone Policies First

Like with computer use, your company may have a strict policy on employees making personal calls on company lines. I know everyone does it, and the occasional call to your fiancé to discuss the caterer you're meeting that evening probably won't land you in the unemployment line — although it could. You may think you can be discreet about your calls, but trust me: once you start talking about your wedding and getting all excited about your upcoming plans,

I'm sure your voice will get louder and more shrill in reaction, and you're bound to draw attention to yourself as you start discussing things like bodices, bridesmaid dresses, and bands. I know this firsthand because I was caught red-handed making wedding-planning calls on company time when I was engaged. I'll never forget the afternoon my boss called me into his office and calmly explained that although he was very excited that I was getting married, he wasn't paying me to write my vows or my invitation copy—that was personal business that should be handled on personal time. Although his admonishment stung at the time, he was right, and that's why I believe you should play it safe.

Chances are you already own a cellular phone. Use it off of company premises for all of your wedding-related calls. That may mean sitting in your car or in a nearby park for your entire lunch hour making calls, but at least this way you won't be risking annoying your boss or coworkers—or damaging your professional reputation or job security—if they overhear your on-premise, wedding-related calls.

> **Wedding Wisdom**
>
> *Many times I would wait until my boss had gone for lunch or was away from her desk, and then I would frantically make phone calls to different vendors. I spent many afternoons racing out of the office to make appointments and meetings. In recent months I hired a wedding coordinator to help with some final details and to also assist on the day of. It has helped a little, but I still handle most of the work on my computer and through quiet phone calls.*
>
> JENNIFER, TEXAS

Schedule Extra Time

If it becomes clear that working on your wedding during the workday is completely taboo, then you're going to have to get creative

Wedding Wisdom

At the time I was planning my wedding, I was working full time and finishing my master's degree. My way of coping and handling all of my responsibilities was to divide my time to be as focused as I could be on one thing at a time. In work, my focus was on my clients and my work. When I needed to make wedding calls, I shut my door at lunchtime, ate very quickly, and then tended to wedding stuff for the remainder of the hour. Then I opened my door and went back to work. I spent my nights and weekends on my studies.

MARISA, NEW JERSEY

about how you're going to keep your job and plan your wedding. Adjusting your schedule and becoming more efficient with your time is your only option. So, if you're normally an early-to-bed or a loves-to-sleep-late person, you're going to have to stay up later or rise earlier to get everything done. That may mean sending all of your E-mails before going to work or before going to bed. Same thing with Web surfing or calls you need to make to members of your wedding party. Most wedding vendors these days have websites, so take advantage of their E-mail option and use it to ask basic questions that you might discuss in a phone conversation during business hours but, thanks to technology, you can E-mail at three in the morning, if need be.

Get Organized

I know a bride who purchased a basic three-ring binder with section dividers and made it her ad hoc wedding-planning book. Whether she was sketching her dream wedding dress while stopped at a red light or jotting down questions she wanted to ask her photographer, she used this book to hold everything she needed to know, ask, research, or investigate to plan her wedding. In addition, she always carried this book with her so that if she found a few free minutes during meetings or appointments, she could accomplish something else on her wedding to-do list. Make your own wedding planner if you'd like or buy one at a bookstore. Just make sure that you designate a central (and portable) location for all of your wedding-planning information so it's easy to find and helps you stay organized.

Wedding Wisdom

How did I plan my wedding without losing my job? My fiancé and I decided to hold the wedding at a hotel that was just across the street from my Washington, D.C., office. The hotel had a wonderful reputation and we liked what they offered us, including the price. But what really made it a lifesaver for me was the fact that I could just walk across the street at lunchtime to work on my wedding plans.

SUSAN, VIRGINIA

Use Your Vacation Time Wisely

If you've been with your employer for some time now, you've probably accrued more vacation time than you know what to do with. Surely you'll want to use some of this vacation time for your honeymoon, but here's a thought: if you've gotten engaged during one calendar year but you'll be getting married in another calendar year, you may have more vacation time at your disposal than you realized. If your earned vacation allotment won't roll over into the next year or you're due some days off, do it before the end of the year. Put in for a week off early in your engagement, and plan to use all of that time to get ahead on your wedding plans. Yes, you'll still have loose ends that need tying up as your wedding date approaches, but this way you can spend some free days being productive and getting a grip on your wedding plans. If you're really lucky, maybe your fiancé will be able to take time off as well.

Devise a Flexible Work Schedule

Ask about switching to a flextime schedule. Sometimes, despite the best-laid plans, a wedding takes on a force greater than one can anticipate. No matter how early you come into work or how late you stay up sending E-mails, you still don't seem to be making any progress on your plans. If your employer offers flextime, see if you can qualify for it. Yes, this kind of work arrangement is usually reserved for working parents or employees dealing with an elder-care situation, but your employee may just go for it.

Many companies in environmentally conscious cities and states receive tax benefits for offering flexible schedules, because these off-hours arrangements help to reduce traffic and thus auto emissions. Your employer may be one of them. Just make sure that you present your case in a way where the benefits to your employer are obvious. Say something like, "By working from eleven to seven each day, I'll have ample time in the morning to take care of personal business, and you can be sure that my time in the office will be 100 percent focused on the tasks at hand." One thing you should not do is demand that your boss switch you to a telecommuting position full time. Yes, this would give you more time to plan your wedding because you would be working from home, but because of this obvious fact, I get the feeling your boss probably won't go for it.

> **Wedding Wisdom**
> *In regard to not losing my job while planning my wedding, I used the Internet a lot, and I did things very quietly so no one knew I was dealing with wedding stuff on company time.*
> MICHELLE,
> MASSACHUSETTS

Get Help

If none of the previously mentioned options work—and you can't afford to quit your job to plan your wedding—you're going to need to find someone to help you get things done. This help can come in different forms.

You could do something simple like splitting up what needs to get done and then delegating certain tasks to whoever can help—your father, fiancé, or maid of honor—all the while being the overseer of your wedding plans.

Another option is you could bite the fiscal bullet and hire a wedding planner. A wedding planner can do as little as working with your caterer to choose a menu or as much as planning every little detail of your wedding, down to suggesting the bridal salons you visit to purchase your gown. (One of my earlier books, *The Portable Wedding Consultant*, has an extensive chapter on hiring a wedding planner, also known as a wedding consultant.)

Sometimes a wedding planner comes automatically with your reception site. For example, hotels and resorts often employ a few planners to work with couples as they plan their weddings, and their services are part of the hotel's fee. If you're looking for one-stop shopping for your wedding—that is, having the ceremony and reception in one place—then a hotel or resort may be your best option. Not only will the planner come as part of the package (of course, ask first to be sure), but also he or she will usually be able to handle all of the other details of the wedding (flowers, entertainment, etc.) through a recommended vendor program.

A third way to get help is to look to family and friends to literally take the planning of your wedding off your hands. Many brides who live in a city other than where they grew up but who are planning a wedding in their hometown may ask a sister, friend, or parent still living there to take on the bulk of the wedding planning, because of proximity and, most importantly, a desire to help out.

Stacey, a public relations executive in Wisconsin, had her mother coordinate her wedding plans in suburban New York. Because Stacey was a principal in a growing company, she knew she couldn't devote the necessary time to planning her wedding. On the other hand, her mother had recently retired from teaching and had a free-enough schedule—and a great aesthetic ability—to do a fantastic job planning Stacey's wedding. To keep Stacey and her fiancé in the loop, Stacey's mother would usually present two to four options for each element of the wedding, from menu selections to flower choices, and give Stacey and her fiancé the final say. This arrangement was wonderful in a number of ways. One, it let Stacey and her mother both feel involved in the wedding planning. Two, it allowed Stacey to maintain her sanity and her job in the months leading up to her wedding. And, three, it gave Stacey and her mother a chance to grow closer, a bond that is evident even years later.

A Postwedding Career Road Map

Once you've figured out exactly how you're going to get your wedding planned, you're going to have to start thinking about your future and how that's going to affect your career road map. I discussed in Chapter 4 why you need to have a family planning plan in place before you walk down the aisle, and one of the ways that plan is going to affect you is with your job. And believe it or not, you're not going to be the only one thinking this way.

Although plenty of women continue working after they are married—and have kids, too—there are also plenty of employers who may look at you differently now that you're getting married. They may begin wondering how long it will be before you quit or get pregnant and go on maternity leave. Legal or not, this bias exists. I discovered this soon after I got married and decided to quit my public relations job—not because we were starting a family but because I wanted to start my own writing business. I was shocked when my seemingly progressive-thinking boss admitted that he didn't think I was going to stick around much longer after my wedding anyway, because most women don't. Yes, his thinking was sexist but also based on reality.

> ### Wedding Wisdom
>
> *I was actually laid off from my dot-com job six months before my wedding. Talk about stress! However, it ended up being the best thing, as I hooked into free-lance work and was thus able to work my schedule around my wedding planning and events. Then, a month before the wedding, I got a great new job.*
>
> SARA, NEW YORK

So, that's why I recommend being proactive about your short-, medium-, and long-term career plans now—whether it's just thinking about those plans or actually discussing them with your boss. If you work in a profession where years of service will affect how well or poorly you progress, you need to think about your plans for the future of your career now. If you've always dreamed about being a partner in your law firm, then taking time off in a few years to have children may not work for you. Either you're going to have to alter your dream, push off the notion of having kids (such as until after you've made partner), or be honest about who is going to be the primary breadwinner in the family and who is going to be the primary caretaker. In the latter situation, you and your fiancé will need to have a heart-to-heart talk about how you'll handle day-care options, should one of you not be willing to stay home full time with the children, as discussed in Chapter 4.

Part of this planning may involve recognizing that the career you're in or your current employer isn't where you think you'll want to be in five or ten years—or where you ultimately want to be when kids come into the picture. If so, then start making small changes now so you can facilitate those wishes later on. For example, if you've always thought you'd like to be a teacher but you ended up in corporate America instead, plan on going back to school now and earning your teaching certificate or master's degree in education so that you can achieve that career goal a few years down the road. Or switch to an employer that offers education benefits or training in the skills you'll need in a couple of years for whatever job or career you think will play a part in your future. Finally, if starting a family is part of your plan, figure out now what kind of benefits either or both of your employers offer for maternity leave, insurance, and the like. If neither of you is working for a company with sufficient work-life strategies in place, think long term and make the move now to a different employer who will give you what you need so that when you do want to have kids, the transition won't be traumatic.

OLD FRIENDS AND YOUR NEW LIFE

Once you've returned from your honeymoon, you may find yourself being pulled in a number of different directions by your friends and family. Obviously, you're going to want to spend time with your new husband, but to maintain your identity, you're going to need to see your friends as well. And although keeping up with your girlfriends is a great way to keep a part of your old self alive, the truth is, you're simply not going to have enough time in a day, week, month, or year to nurture as many friendships as you once did.

"You need to sit down with your fiancé and figure out which are the friendships you'll want to maintain in your married life," says Anthony Jurich, Ph.D., a marriage and family therapy expert at Kansas State University in Manhattan, Kansas. It's important to do this exercise with your fiancé because this way you're communicating your friendship priorities with each other and not sweeping any secrets under the rug. For example, if your fiancé tells you that he wants to maintain his friendship with his drinking buddies and go barhopping with them every Saturday night, this gives you the opportunity to respond in a number of ways—plus opens a dialogue for communication and compromise. You could say, "Fine, I'll make sure that I make plans with my barhopping girlfriends for Saturday night," and then you've both made it clear that these friendships with your drinking and barhopping buddies are a top priority for you both. Or, you might respond, "Gee, does it have to be every Saturday night? I was hoping we could make Saturday nights our movie-going night," at which point you'll need to figure out a compromise, such as that he'll see his drinking buddies one Saturday night a month or you'll go to the movies one Saturday night a month. Or, you may respond, "Gee, having you go out with those guys makes me uncomfortable. All they want to do is get smashed and pick up girls." At this point, your fiancé should reassure you that although his friends may be interested in that, he's not. He just wants to hang out with them. It's up to you to determine if you trust him and can live with his decision to continue seeing those friends under those circumstances.

"Friendships usually fall into three categories. They are, 'I want to keep this friend no matter what.' Then there is 'This is a friend that I have now and will probably drop off in the next few years.'

> **Wedding Wisdom**
>
> *My fiancé and I decided that we weren't going to be one of those couples that is completely engrossed in wedding planning. We've tried to separate our social life from too many conversations about the wedding, for our sanity and our friends' sanity as well.*
>
> TEREZ, NEW YORK

Finally, there are 'These are the friendships that aren't worth nurturing,'" says Dr. Jurich. Because your social time is finite, you'll need to qualify each of your friendships, see where they fall in each of these categories, and then see whether you can make them work in your new life together.

Sometimes the solution is simple: "I've been to so many college graduations where you think that the people sitting next to you are the most important people in the world and that you'll always be friends," says Dr. Jurich. Of course, in most instances, the reality is this: once you've moved away from each other and are no longer sharing an experience on a day-to-day basis, such as going to college together, working in the same office, or hitting the single bars as a group, your friendship will normally fade.

Sometimes the reality is heartbreaking—that the girlfriend you thought would always be there for you has grown cold and distant now that you're engaged. Your first course of action should be trying to figure out what's going on in the friendship. Ask the girlfriend who has grown distant, "Have I done something to upset you?" or "Is everything OK with you?" If these attempts don't generate a satisfying response nor seem to mend any broken bonds, then you've got to let that friendship go. Your priority should be in nurturing your relationship with your soon-to-be new husband, not a friendship with a jealous, spiteful, or incommunicative person.

Then, of course, there are the friendships that can withstand your getting married and possibly moving away. These are the kind of relationships where the person never questions your commitment or gives you a hard time when a couple of months have passed without a phone call. In an ideal situation, this person goes from a single friend of yours to a friend to both of you, and then to a couple friend when he or she finds a mate and marries.

BLENDING YOUR FAMILIES

When Stacey, the public relations executive I mentioned earlier, married Stuart, their wedding brought their respective parents together to get to know one another, but on their own, their parents developed a unique friendship that has grown beyond simply being in-laws. Now, they even travel together. Something similar happened with my and my husband's mothers. Beyond getting to know one another because their children were marrying, each went out of her way to invite the other to family-oriented occasions at each other's home. If my mother was hosting Thanksgiving one year, she was sure to invite my mother-in-law to join us. If my mother-in-law was planning an elaborate Christmas dinner, she always set a place for my mother and invited her to join us for the celebration. Although I wouldn't say that these two have become the best of friends, they keep in touch despite their now living in faraway states. This friendship has allowed Bill and me to feel a part of a bigger family that isn't divided by bloodlines but rather is joined by a common bond—the marriage of their children.

Maybe you'll be lucky, and your respective parents will get along wonderfully from the start. Or perhaps you come from different religious backgrounds, so celebrating family holidays will never be a cause of conflict because they don't overlap. But, sooner or later, you're going to have to figure out what to do with holidays like Thanksgiving, which everyone celebrates, or when you have kids, how you'll handle vacations that include visits to see your parents. As I've said time and time again, the key to a happy marriage—including when it involves your respective parents—is communication and compromise. So, early on in your relationship, create situations where your parents can get to know one another and, ideally, start a dialogue with one another.

Furthermore, during your engagement, set some examples of how you're going to handle family situations in the years to come by talking about possible conflicts now. For example, if both sets of parents expect that you'll be spending Christmas Eve with them every year, make it clear that you want to spend the holidays with your families, but that by getting married, you're becoming a family, too. Suggest ways of making everyone feel acknowledged and meeting their needs, such as by having both sets of parents visit you on Christmas. Or, if your parents live nearby, figure out a way to see one on Christmas Eve and then the other on Christmas Day. The last thing you should be doing on holidays is running yourself ragged from house to house, just to please your parents. They need to compromise, too, and the only way for you to determine what will work best is to talk about it. In addition, by encouraging a friendship between your parents, if that's possible, you've created a way for them to talk directly about possible scheduling conflicts and save you two from always being caught in the middle of every parent-oriented discussion.

Wedding Wisdom
I always made time for family and friends during the planning process, doing things that they wanted to do. I've seen brides who've taken the "queen for a day" theory and stretched it to "queen for six to eight months before the wedding." It's easy to become self-absorbed, and that can be damaging to the people around you.

GWEN, NEW JERSEY

WHEN BECOMING A STEPPARENT IS PART OF THE DEAL

In many of today's marriages, one or both of the partners have been married before. According to the Stepfamily Association of America, 43 percent of all marriages are remarriages, and of these remarriages, 65 percent of them involve children from the prior marriage. If this statistic describes your situation, then you know that when you marry each other, not only are you becoming husband and wife, but you may also be taking on the title of stepfather or stepmother. For you, your husband, and any involved children to make a smooth transition into this life, you need to understand that not everything is going to be perfect from the moment you say, "I do."

Claire Berman is the author of *Making It as a Stepparent* (Doubleday, 1986) and former president of the Stepfamily Association of America. She says that there are two things people need to recognize up front about stepfamilies. First, a stepfamily will never replicate a first family. And, second, a stepfamily can be an uncomfortable situation at the start—with everyone self-conscious of who is saying what to whom and in what tone of voice. In addition, "A regular marriage has a honeymoon period, where you can be intimate and alone," says Berman. "With a stepfamily, there is an immediate audience, so intimacy issues can be hard to deal with. You want to say, 'I'm the new bride and I want to be the first woman you're with,' but with someone who has been married before, that's not a reality." Sometimes, Berman says, children who look like or remind the person of their spouse's ex can really make the adjustment period difficult. But what it comes down to is this: if you're not prepared to welcome these children into your life, your marriage may not survive.

So how can you make the transition from new bride or groom to stepmother or stepfather? Berman offers these tips:

• *Don't expect instant love.* Your primary responsibility as husband and wife is to love one another. In addition, you have to be decent to each other's children and include them in your life as much as possible. They, in turn, must be decent to you. If love happens to come as part of that package, then you're very lucky, but don't expect it. It's the exception, not the rule.

- *Don't try to replace an original parent.* Regardless of how motherly or fatherly you are to your spouse's children, you will never be a substitute for their mother or father. The only time this replacement role ever happens—and it's rare even then—is when children are very young and their mother or father has died.

- *Give your spouse time alone with the kids.* The worst thing a new stepparent can do is demand that all the time her spouse spends with his kids must involve her as well. This is especially important if the original parent has more than one child. You can arrange to have one of the children spend the morning going shopping with you while your spouse takes his other child to the Little League game. What you don't want, though, is your stepchildren always asking to be with their parent alone. Just as they have become a part of your lives, you are a part of theirs and they need to accept that. Never doing anything with you won't bode well for the future of your relationship—especially if your spouse allows it.

- *Ascertain the role money will play in your job as a stepparent—and in the lives of any stepchildren.* For many children of divorce, being given money or having a parent buy them things oftentimes equals love. If your husband's young son always asks for you to buy him something whenever he's with you, think about where this request is coming from. He's probably just looking for a material validation of his parent's love, not being a spoiled child. So, in the long run, will it really kill you to buy him the ninety-nine-cent trinket? Probably not. But don't try to buy his love just to appease him. Instead, if you're going to spend money on your stepchild, buy something you can enjoy doing together, such as modeling clay or the latest Harry Potter book.

From the stepparent's perspective, you need to be clear from the start how each person's income will affect the parent's support of his or her children. In some instances, the birth parent earns enough that tapping into the stepparent's take-home pay isn't an issue. But if it seems like your combined income will be jointly supporting the other person's kid—and you think you're going to have an issue with it—get it out in the open now. "If you're going to stew each month when the check goes out, you're going to be bitter, terrible to live with, and always fighting with your spouse," says Berman. "So if this issue is a deal breaker now, it will be a deal breaker down the line."

When you marry someone with children, you must welcome those children in your life and be willing to deal with whatever comes down the pike. If that means dealing with financial issues, then you have to understand that money will be part of the deal. That's not to say that you have to become a financial doormat. It's perfectly reasonable for you to say, "I'm more than happy to help support your children, but I don't want to do so at the detriment of our own well-being. So I'm going to take X of my income each month and set it aside for us." If your future husband has a problem with your doing this, then you're going to have to figure out a financial compromise before you walk down the aisle.

• *Seriously consider going for premarital counseling—either alone, together, or with the kids.* This is especially important in remarriage situations because, statistically, your marriage is more likely to fail than to succeed: according to the Stepfamily Association of America, 60 percent of remarriages end in divorce. To beat the odds, you're going to have to work even harder at your relationship. Premarital counseling, even for the short term, is a good idea for anyone getting married. But for those who have been divorced or are marrying someone who is divorced, it's a chance to get everything out in the open about why the first marriage failed and what you can do as a couple to ensure that this marriage succeeds.

• *Involve the children in the wedding.* Nothing is more welcoming to a child whose mother or father is remarrying than taking part in the wedding itself. The important thing to remember is you need to involve that child only as much or as little as that child feels comfortable doing. You may be all excited about having his daughter be your flower girl, but the idea of it may freak her out. So, together let her know how you'd like her to participate in the wedding, but leave the decision up to her. Give her a deadline for letting you know what she wants to do, and then accept whatever she decides. By reaching out to her at the wedding, you'll be getting your relationship off on the right foot. If she agrees to be the flower girl, great. If she doesn't, make sure that you at least list her and any of your respective kids in the program. That way, even if they're not standing up there with you, you're recognizing them in some way.

• *Cultivate some sort of relationship with your soon-to-be spouse's ex-spouse.* Regardless of how difficult or unpleasant this suggestion seems, having lines of communication open with an ex-spouse will help when the children stay with you and try to pull the wool over your eyes because they figure you don't know any better. So, when the kids reach for the remote before they've finished their homework—and you know this is not allowed in their home—you can say, "Hey, guys, I've spoken with your mom, and I know that she doesn't let you watch TV before homework." Yes, this might set you up as the bad guy in the short term, but in the long run it will benefit everyone. Think about it this way: if you maintain the mother's rules in your home, the children will come home behaving well, and all of you will be working together as a team to raise these children the same way. But if you let them get away with everything when they stay with you because you don't want to cause waves, they'll go back to their mother saying things like, "Well, Dad's wife lets us do this and that," and that will just increase any animosity that may be simmering below the surface.

• *If the children will be living with you, don't settle down after marriage in the same house where they once lived with the other parent.* Regardless of whether that parent died or got divorced, "In a house there are always ghosts of relationships past," says Berman. "Buying a new bed or replacing the furniture doesn't do the job as well as buying a new home. The people who lived there before will always be the residents, and the new spouse will always be the intruder." When you buy the new house, try to stay in the same neighborhood or, with school-age children, at least the same school district, so there won't be too much change at once for the children. But do whatever you have to do financially to make buying a new house a reality.

For more information on making stepfamilies work, contact the Stepfamily Association of America at 800-735-0329 or log onto stepfam.org.

BALANCE: THE BOTTOM LINE

One of the worst things that could happen to you as you plan your wedding is getting fired. I'm not talking about downsizing due to the economy, but rather negligence on your part: letting your wedding become such an all-consuming matter that you can't do your job anymore and lose it. To avoid ending up in the unemployment line during your engagement, use the strategies in this chapter to plan your wedding without losing your job—or, for that matter, losing your mind.

Another thing that you risk losing when you get married are friends. These soon-to-be former friends could be jealous of your getting married or simply at a place in life that no longer matches yours. Your time is already limited by your wedding plans and will be limited afterward as well while you spend time bonding with your new husband. It's important for you to recognize that the ebb and flow of friendship is normal and to prepare for any friendships that may fall out of favor in the coming months and years.

With so many weddings involving remarriage, chances are that when you say, "I do," not only will you become your husband's wife, but you may also become someone's stepmother—or your fiancé becomes a stepfather. I've provided a number of ways to help you and your fiancé build, not force, a relationship with any stepchildren you may be welcoming into your marriage. You may not end up with everything peachy-keen like the utterly unrealistic "Brady Bunch," but this advice will provide a good start to what should be a very happy life together.

Part III

SPIRIT

9

A FRESH START

WHEN SUSAN MET Henry, he was just coming out of a failed relationship. This was no mere breakup, though: Henry had just finalized a divorce from his first wife. All of Susan's friends told her that Henry was bad news, that she should avoid dating him, and that she would just end up being his rebound girlfriend—only to be dumped weeks, maybe months, later. But Susan ignored their warnings because she saw something worthwhile in Henry and their possible future together. Despite dealing with a failed marriage after less than a year of matrimony, Henry spoke warmly about marrying again, starting a family, and trying to get things right in a future marriage. In addition, he was seeing a counselor, a good sign in her book, and, most importantly, he talked openly with Susan about his first marriage and the events that had led to its demise.

"What I grew to love about Henry was the fact that his past wasn't a closed book as it seemed to have been with every other man I'd ever dated," says Susan, who shared the successes and failures from her own past relationships with Henry as well. Over time, the two of them did a pretty good job of outlining their own relationship strengths and weaknesses, and they learned to use their past to help craft a road map for their future together. For example, they determined that for Henry to feel he was an important part of their duo, he needn't kowtow to Susan's every wish and desire, something he'd done in his first marriage, mostly to avoid causing conflict. Through therapy, he'd come to see that his constantly keeping quiet caused more problems than prevented them. Likewise, Susan learned that when things weren't going well, leaving the situation—either physically or emotionally—wasn't the solution.

"In my parents' marriage, which ended in divorce, every time there was a fight, someone would storm out of the room before things got resolved," Susan recalls. "As an adult, I'd do the same thing with my boyfriends. If we started arguing, I would suddenly need to run to the store or I would start daydreaming and just 'check out' of the situation. Or I would let my yelling escalate to the point that I literally forced my boyfriend to leave the room, just so he could escape from me and my mania. With Henry, though, I realized that arguing over stuff was OK and not every disagreement had to end in a huff."

As Susan and Henry worked to come to terms with what made their past relationships fail—and how their parents' interactions

Wedding Wisdom

We both had previous relationships that were serious, but then went awry for one reason or another. We spent many nights in the beginning of the relationship talking about our pasts so that neither of us would be surprised about things that would come up in the future. We both tried to view past relationships as important stepping-stones to get us to where we are today and that the past really helped us become who we are and ultimately to end up together.

SARAH, ILLINOIS

affected them in ways they never realized—their bond with one another strengthened. Not surprisingly, they soon fell in love. Nearly two years to the day after they met, they got engaged and, a year later, they were married.

Exorcising Your Relationship Demons

Henry and Susan were smart. They knew that although the past may not have been pleasant, it was a big part of *who* they were as adults and affected *how* they interacted with one another. Perhaps you may not think that any of your old boyfriends or past partners will affect you in your current relationship with your fiancé, but guess what? They will, and if you don't address at least some of the stuff that has happened with other partners in the past, then you are sure to have some serious relationship issues in the future. That's because sooner or later, one of those relationship demons will rear its ugly head. Then, in a matter of seconds, you may find yourself having the same fight that you had with a former boyfriend or spouse or perhaps witnessed your parents having years ago. Or, you may experience your partner reacting unexpectedly and inappropriately to a casual comment. You won't know where his rage or negative energy is coming from, but come forth it will. Let me tell you how avoiding the past affected Tina and Jerry, an engaged couple.

One day after work Tina went shopping with her girlfriends and bought some new clothes. She was very excited about her purchase and couldn't wait to show off her new duds to Jerry. Although Tina had a small twinge of guilt about her shopping spree, because she and Jerry had been on a bit of self-imposed austerity to help them save for the wedding, Tina reasoned that this little splurge, her first ever, wouldn't have a huge effect on their spending ability. And in the grand scheme of things, her $100 expenditure probably wouldn't have hurt their long-term savings plan, but it did almost hurt her relationship—and not because of any fault of Tina's.

That evening when Tina told Jerry about her shopping adventure and asked if he would like for her to model her new clothes, Jerry simply exploded. "The next thing I knew Jerry was talking about spendthrift women, how they just take men for all they have, and how my out-of-control spending was going to ruin us," recalls Tina, who says that Jerry ranted on and on for many minutes. "It was when he called me by his ex-girlfriend's name that I had an inkling of what was really going on."

What *was* going on was this: Tina had unknowingly hit one of Jerry's raw nerves—the uncontrollable spending habits of his former girlfriend. Tina had suspected this was the downfall of Jerry's previous relationship, but she never knew for sure. That's because Jerry hadn't been willing to talk about his relationship with this ex-girlfriend—or any of his ex-girlfriends, for that matter. Although this was troubling to Tina, she had let Jerry's timidity of talking about the past go—that is, until the night of the explosion.

"I found myself screaming right back at him, 'I'm not Karen. I'm not Karen,' who was his previous girlfriend," says Tina. After a few minutes, Jerry calmed down enough to realize his mistake, and that's when Tina told him that he really needed to start telling her what had gone wrong in his relationship with Karen and possibly what he was worried might go wrong in their relationship as well. This was a healthy start for Tina and Jerry to exorcise the demons of his past relationships.

When I talk about exorcising these demons, I'm not saying that you have to spell out the details of all of your past sexual escapades or give a blow-by-blow of your previous marriage. Instead, talking about what happened with other partners in general terms is a way of dealing with the past and coming away with a stronger sense of who you are, what makes you happy in a relationship, and what you are looking for in your future marriage to this person.

"If you had a marriage that didn't work out, then you better have learned something from that experience—and be able to share it with your new partner," says Susan Perry, Ph.D., a social psychologist who is researching a book on long-term happy marriages. In addition, "I've seen relationships start and then fizzle out when the partners say that they don't want to talk about the past because it's a closed book. Well, I think that you're missing out on a very important chance to talk about all of those things that happened in that so-called closed book."

You've got to understand that these experiences from that "closed book" shape who you are today and how you'll behave in your current relationship. Mind you, talking about the past isn't going to be easy.

One of the biggest challenges of talking about the past is how easy it is to stumble into sensitive territory. You may find your fiancé waxing wistfully for the town where he and his previous girlfriend lived, or you could accidentally hurt the one you love by unconsciously comparing past and present partners.

Sometimes it's the mere thought of a previous partner or spouse that doesn't sit well with you or your fiancé. That's OK, and you need to let the other person know that so you can talk about it. Although it's important to hear what happened in that past marriage and what he hopes to do differently in this new marriage, it's also all right to let him know that every so often during your talk, you'd like him to remind you that he loves you now and wants to marry you for all of these great reasons, which he can list. This will help you each feel loved and wanted as you stroll—carefully—down memory lane.

YOUR EMERGING AND EVOLVING RELATIONSHIP

One of the absolutes of being in a relationship is that it will change over time. As you experience things together, you grow closer, and as you grow closer, your relationship becomes more intimate. If your relationship didn't evolve, it wouldn't last.

"I hear too many couples say something like, 'You've really changed,'" says Rebecca Ward, a couples' therapist in Little Rock, Arkansas, and author of *How to Stay Married Without Going Crazy* (Rainbow Books, 2000). "But I don't think people really change. Rather they've begun to be more authentic because they're comfortable in the marriage, and they don't feel the need to 'hide' stuff anymore."

It's the hiding of stuff that can lead to trouble. So many couples are afraid of conflict that they'll hide their feelings and continually placate one another in difficult situations, but this can only work in the short term. "If something is annoying you on a regular basis, you've got to bring it up," says Dr. Perry. If you don't, you'll only harbor resentment, and you'll never be able to get past whatever it was that was bothering you.

One of the areas of a relationship that tends to cause the most conflict—and that one or both partners feels unjustified in bringing up for discussion—is the roles that you unconsciously expect one another to assume. If I may get psychoanalytical on you for a second, this issue goes back to our parents' relationships and how they dealt with the roles and responsibilities that come with being married. There are plenty of role-related minefields that you may accidentally step on as you plan your wedding—and that you must protect against detonating by defusing them immediately. Here are some common trouble areas, their triggers, and how to deal with them:

- *"It's her wedding anyway."* Yes, it's true that most women—even the most modern among us—have been daydreaming about their weddings since they were little girls. Watch any five-year-old female at play, and you'll quickly realize the prominent part getting married plays in pretend fun. Fast forward a couple of decades and that grown-up girl is getting married for real. Her fiancé is probably acutely aware that his love has been planning her wedding in her mind for years, so he just backs off and says, "Whatever you want, dear, is fine with me." Even though that seems like the best way to deal with things and avoid conflict at the same time, it's not a good precedent to set. Too often a couple sees the wedding-planning time as a free pass from real life. "They say things like 'When this (the wedding) is over, we can settle down and get on with things,'" says Dr. Perry, but "this" is the beginning of the rest of your life. If you don't learn how to deal with issues now, you'll have a rude awakening a few weeks, months, or years down the line. In these kinds of relationships, couples who have pushed off reality for as long as they can may end up saying, "You're not the person I thought you were when we got married." If you want a clearer sense of exactly who your fiancé is going to be as your husband and what he'll be like to deal with "until death do you part," then deal with conflict now; don't avoid it.

- *"That's the man's/woman's job."* Very early on in the wedding-planning process, you'll see a division of gender—whether it's who's going to pick the flowers or the photographer or who's managing the money you're saving for your wedding. Much of this goes back to your parents and how they divided tasks. "Who held the power? Who made the decisions? How did they deal with money issues?" asks Ward. The answers to these questions will help you decide how you're going to negotiate who does what in your marriage. Sometimes you'll come to an agreement with very little negotiating, and other times you may have to negotiate every little thing. "If you're doing all the housecleaning and he says that a clean home is not important to him, then you've got to figure out a middle ground," says Dr. Perry. "Either he has to do more around the house to please you and you will accept his help, or you must accept the fact that you have different values about a clean house, that housecleaning will probably fall on your shoulders, and you can't resent him for those differences."

Working out who will clean the house is a perfect example of the day-to-day negotiations you should expect as you plan your wedding and move into married life together. As far as the wedding goes, you can get off on the right negotiation foot by sitting down and asking each other, "OK, what do you want at our wedding?" Recognize that what he wants may not be the same thing that you want, and vice versa, and that's OK. The important thing is to talk about it, hear each other out, and then figure out something that sits well with both of you.

THE PARENT TRAP

So, what is it about your parents' relationship that affects how you perform in your own relationships? Basically, they offered you the blueprint for all that is good—and bad—in being with someone else. Watching your parents taught you how to talk about stuff, how to show affection, how to resolve conflict (if at all), and much more. "So much of this is unconscious, and you don't even know that you have these opinions or habits until you're in the throes of marriage," says Ward, whose book includes questions you can ask yourself to help reveal your own parents' traps—and how you can avoid becoming ensnared in them in your own marriage.

One thing that is inevitable is that you will replicate your parents' relationship, regardless of how many times you say "I will not become my mother or father." But, if you work at it, you can avoid ending up with all of their negative relationship qualities. Rather, you can highlight what you liked or admired about your parents' interactions with one another and work at having that in your marriage. For example, if your parents were openly affectionate with one another and that always gave you the warm fuzzies, being openly affectionate with your fiancé is probably something you'll want to strive for. In addition, there may be personality traits about each parent that you may have unknowingly looked for in a partner—and found in your fiancé. That's great because, as Ward explains, it puts you in a "similar emotional milieu" and attributes to feelings of happiness and being content. The only times that these traits are troublesome is when you come from a verbally or physically abusive family and end up replicating that abuse in the relationship you have with your fiancé. That's when counseling—and possibly postponing your wedding—comes into play.

Conversely, if your parents' marriage ended in divorce, it's perfectly reasonable for you to go into your marriage thinking that divorce is not an option—and then working hard to keep your marriage strong so that you don't end up divorced like your parents.

SIX WAYS TO MAKE
YOUR MARRIAGE STRONGER

Even though you're not married yet, how you get through planning your wedding is a great prelude to how successful your marriage will be. Here are six things you can learn to do today that will make your marriage stronger tomorrow—and for years to come.

1. Communicate

You can't expect to get what you want in a marriage or be happy with the choices you make in any of the areas of your life if you don't communicate your feelings. Although it might seem silly to bring up how your fiancé puts the toilet paper on the roll, if this is an issue for you, you need to deal with it. For one couple, Mark and Kim, it was.

Mark's family has owned and operated a chain of restaurants for three decades. It was in the kitchen of his family's restaurant where Mark spent his formative years, although one of his first jobs was stocking the restaurant's paper goods, including toilet paper. "My father always told me that the proper way for toilet paper to unroll is over the top. So, this is how I've always done it," he says. Kim, on the other hand, never received lessons in the fine art of refilling toilet paper, so when she needed to replace a roll, she just popped it in. A few weeks after moving in together, Mark told Kim he needed to talk to her. He sat her down and said that it was really bothering him how she was refilling the toilet paper. "He started discussing why toilet paper should go over the top and not come underneath, and, frankly, I couldn't believe that we were talking about this," says Kim. "I mean, we're sitting on the couch discussing toilet paper! But then I realized that despite my just seeing this as one of Mark's obsessive issues, it was also something that was important to Mark but wasn't to me." So, what happened? Kim told Mark that she would do her best to refill the toilet paper the right way, but for the most part she would leave that job up to him. This was a fine compromise for Mark, and they never fought over toilet paper again. As silly as this scenario seems because of the toilet-paper connection, it's an excellent example of how communication—or nipping a problem in the bud or before it gets blown out of proportion—can only help your relationship.

The Lighter Side: A Truce in the Toilet War

One of the longest-running bathroom-related battles of the sexes involves the toilet seat—should a man put the toilet seat down after using the loo or should his wife look before sitting so she doesn't have a "splash-down"? To help call a truce in the toilet wars, there's the Johnny-Light, a small green light that tucks under the toilet rim and is activated when the seat goes up. That way even a bleary-eyed husband taking a middle-of-the-night bathroom break can't help but notice this gentle, green reminder to put the seat down. The Johnny-Light costs approximately $12 and is available at Lowe's Home Improvement stores. You can also order it by calling 888-566-LITE (5483) or logging onto Johnny-light.com.

2. Take Responsibility for Yourself and Your Actions

One of the reasons that Mark and Kim were able to get over the toilet-paper incident was because Mark owned up to the fact that toilet paper was his problem, not Kim's. He didn't try to place any blame on Kim or say that she had done anything wrong. Beyond toilet paper, taking responsibility means you can't blame your partner for your quirks, idiosyncrasies, or, in the bigger picture, the choices that you did or didn't make in your life. For example, if your fiancé wants to take a job in a new city after you get married and you don't love the idea, yet you don't raise any objections, you can't turn around and blame him for your loneliness six months down the road because you don't know anyone in this new place. If you had issues with moving, you should have raised them before you packed any boxes. Now, this doesn't mean that you should sit there and wallow in feeling miserable. Go back to rule one and communicate your feelings. It may not result in your moving back to your city of origin tomorrow, but it will help you feel better. Then, together brainstorm ways for you to feel happier in your new place. Or the two of you may decide that you need to set a timeline for moving back and work together toward meeting that goal.

3. Acknowledge Your Partner's Feelings

It's never good to tell someone what they think or feel is stupid or ridiculous, as Kim was tempted to do in the toilet-paper incident. That's not helpful, just hurtful. "Rather, it's better to say, 'I hear you, and I'm sorry you feel like that' or 'I bet that's painful for you,' even when you're saying inside that this is the nuttiest thing you've ever heard," says Ward. Once you've acknowledged your partner's feel-

ings, you can work toward finding a way of making him feel better—
and avoiding these hurt feelings again in the future.

4. Don't Keep Score

One of the predictors of a happy marriage is that both partners feel
that they're getting out of the relationship what they're putting into
it. If you are starting to feel as if the burden pendulum is not swing-
ing in your favor, speak up. You shouldn't go through your married
life—or the engagement period, for that matter—with an imaginary
scorecard in your head, marking down all of the times he wasn't fair
or didn't do his fair share of the housework. A marriage should be an
equal partnership with an intuitive feeling of things being equitable.
If you don't feel this way already, work on communicating your feelings better, and, if that doesn't work, seek professional counseling.

5. Build Bonds of Playfulness

"What is so unique about each couple and makes you irreplaceable
to each other is how you laugh and have fun together," says Dr.
Perry. In addition, laughter can be a great anger diffuser when things
aren't going well. For example, over the years my husband Bill has
learned that the fastest and easiest way to get me out of a bad mood
is to tickle me. He reasons that when you're laughing, you can't be
mad. And you know what? He's right. In addition, we've discovered
that when we're in the midst of an argument that seems to be head-
ing down the road to nowhere, if one of us does something funny,
we can immediately get our anger in check and start talking all over
again. I'll never forget the time right after we'd gotten engaged and
were dealing with some wedding-related issue that was fraught with
emotion. Our discussion was quickly turning into an argument

when Bill walked over to the sink, filled a glass of water, and dumped it over his head. I couldn't help but laugh and ask him, "Why on earth did you do that?" to which he replied, "I needed to cool down." He then continued that he thought I needed to cool down and asked if he could dump a glass of water on my head, too. I giggled, "Yes," and after dousing me, our moods immediately improved. Later, when we'd changed into dry clothes, we were able to resume our wedding talk and, thanks to our cooler heads, come up with a solution that was pleasing all around.

6. Focus on the Positive

Sometimes in the craziness that accompanies planning a wedding, you simply forget what all of this hard work is for—you're marrying someone you love and want to spend the rest of your life with. That's why it's a good exercise to take time every so often and list all of the things that are wonderful about your fiancé, why you love him, and why you want to be his wife. Of course, if you've got some negatives, you can list them, too, because listing them may present an excellent opportunity to communicate any issues that may have been annoying you. But the bottom line is, the positives should always outweigh the negatives. Adds Dr. Perry, "If they don't, you've got no business going any further with your wedding plans."

CONSIDER PREMARITAL COUNSELING

It may seem that only those couples who are having unresolved issues need premarital counseling, but the truth is, every engaged couple could benefit from at least one session with a marriage and family therapist. "Most of the happy couples who have been married for the long term have seen a counselor at least briefly, either individually or together," says Dr. Perry. Sometimes as little as two sessions are all a couple needs to get on the path of communication and conflict resolution, two of the most common areas that people don't know how to do well. In addition, you should think of premarital counseling like preventative health care. We now know that the best way to treat our body is not to be reactive in only treating symptoms as they occur but rather to be proactive in maintaining our good health long term so that we can avoid illness. Why not be proactive about your relationship health as well?

One reason that couples can benefit from premarital counseling is this: every newly married couple goes through the same stages of postwedding disillusionment. That is, two days, two months, or two years after your wedding, you're going to turn around and say, "What did I get myself into?" or "You're not who I thought you were when

---

Wedding Wisdom

As a way of getting premarital counseling, we signed up for an "Engaged Encounter" weekend organized by the Catholic Church. It ended up being one of the best weekends we ever spent. It wasn't overly religious, but we did talk about spirituality. The facilitators would speak for a few minutes on trust, previous relationships, family, religion, and other topics. Then each couple would spend a few minutes individually writing his/her thoughts and then get together in private rooms to share their writings. We learned a lot about each other that weekend, and have a written record of how we felt about life, the universe, and everything prior to our marriage. We both felt a lot more confident in our relationship after the weekend.

HEATHER, MASSACHUSETTS

I married you," and those reactions are perfectly normal. "If you've discussed this possibility with a counselor and how to deal with it when it happens, it won't catch you by surprise," says Dr. Perry. "On the other hand, if you expect that everything is going to be wonderful and will go on that way forever and ever, when it doesn't, you won't know what to do."

Counseling can also help by opening up a discussion about your past relationships as well as your parents' relationship, if you haven't already been over this territory, and allow you to talk about these issues in a safe environment. "Understand, you're not going to counseling to be talked out of marrying someone but simply to see how helpful it can be to talk to a third party about your relationship," adds Dr. Perry. "Also, ideally the counselor will be on the side of the two of you having a good, long happy relationship." If you find that your counselor is attempting to pit one of you against the other, however, it's time to seek out another counselor.

Now, if you or your fiancé are scared to go into a therapy setting and address your current relationship, or if you've had a wedding-related fight that you can't resolve, these are both clear-cut reasons that you really ought to seek out premarital counseling and fast. If you're facing serious stumbling blocks in your wedding plans, or, worse, your relationship, you've got to figure out a way to resolve these issues—even if one of you is afraid of going into therapy—or postpone the wedding. Your future happiness may depend on it.

BALANCE: THE BOTTOM LINE

The cool thing about being in love and having an ongoing relationship with someone is how that relationship evolves over time—and evolve it will. There is no such thing as a successful *and* static relationship. Current events affect the nature of your relations, including the planning of your wedding. So do past events, such as previous relationships you've had or the interactions (both positive and negative) you've witnessed between your parents. All of these things form who you are, how you love, and the roles you play in a relationship. That's why talking about the past, present, and future is critical to the success of your marriage: your fiancé needs to know where you've been, where you are now, and where you hope to go in the future (in your marriage and beyond).

Because a marriage should last a lifetime, this chapter has served up six ways to make your marriage stronger so that, ideally, it will endure until death do you part. These strengthening exercises included building bonds of playfulness and accentuating the positive. However, should you need extra help, there's premarital counseling—a good plan for engaged couples, simply to help open the lines of communication, a critical element in any successful relationship. Remember: getting professional help doesn't necessarily mean something is wrong. Sometimes, in fact, it's the opposite—a sign that things are so right between you that you've recognized you could use an objective third party to help strengthen and solidify your relationship.

10

RELIGION AND YOUR FUTURE FAMILY

To MY HUSBAND, Bill, and me, it was glaringly obvious that before we got engaged, let alone married, we needed to have "the talk." What do I mean by "the talk?" No, not about sex but a talk about religion. You see, I was raised Jewish, and Bill was raised Roman Catholic. We knew that if we were to come together to form a family one day, we would have to make some clear decisions about which religion we would choose as our family's primary one. Sure, we could have taken the easy route out and tried to celebrate holidays and follow customs of both religions. Or, we could have attempted to meld our religions into some kind of new-fangled amalgamation of Judaism and Catholicism. Or, we could have been paralyzed by our differences and done nothing at all. However, based on the people we knew who married into or were raised in a "mixed" marriage, we'd seen firsthand how each of those three scenarios could be brought to life. Frankly, we didn't like any of the outcomes we'd witnessed, and so we knew we had to do something different.

For example, we have a friend from high school who has a Jewish mother and a Protestant father, and she grew up neither Jewish nor Christian. Her parents hadn't pushed either of their religions onto her or her siblings because they wanted to leave the religion decision up to their children for when they became adults. Yes, her family had gone through the motions of celebrating many of the major religious holidays of each faith—Christmas, Hanukkah, and Easter—but there was never a higher meaning to any of these celebrations. Add to that the fact that our friend's parents hadn't presented any sort of spirituality at all during her formative years—talk of God was practically verboten under their roof and the family attended neither synagogue or church—and it's no surprise she grew up feeling as if she had no affinity to any religion. This left her without a spiritual persona, and if you were to ask our friend today what religion she is, she would tell you, "Nothing."

Of course, there is the flip side to this story: another couple we know have a "mixed marriage," and they tried to celebrate all of the holidays from both Judaism and Christianity, but they never did it as a team effort, which seemed like a terrible example for their four children. Here's how their December holiday scenario would go. The dad, who was Jewish, was OK with having a Christmas tree in the house and decorations throughout, but he would have nothing to do with the choosing, buying, or setting up of them. That was left for the mom, who was Catholic. Even the year that the mom managed to get a great deal on a nine-foot tree—but had trouble setting it up—the dad wouldn't help her because, as he said aloud like he did every December, that Christmas wasn't "his" holiday. Likewise, on Hanukkah, the dad would light the menorah candles with the four children and say the blessing, but the mom would be nowhere around. She wanted nothing to do with prayers said in Hebrew. If you only visited this house once on a holiday, you would easily see which were the "mom" holidays and which were the "dad" holidays. But, short of Thanksgiving, you'd never witness a "family" holiday. How could their children not be aware of the religious dividing line in that household? I've never been to that home on Christmas morn-ing, but I wouldn't be surprised to learn that none of the packages under the tree were from "Mom and Dad"—probably just from the mom, because Christmas was "her" holiday.

Bill and I knew that we didn't want to end up a family divided by religion either. So, one evening many months before we were engaged, we broached the subject of religion. We talked extensively about our experiences growing up with our respective religions—me attending Hebrew school two days a week for many years, plus Friday night and Saturday morning services at synagogue; him going through religious classes at his Catholic church, plus attending mass weekly with his family. Some of our discussions involved fond remembrances of holidays spent with family as well as disdain for certain religious rit-uals to which we had to submit. We talked so much about our reli-gious experiences and opinions that the conversation continued for a long time—we'd pick it up after work and then again after dinner, and on it went for many weeks.

> **Wedding Wisdom**
> *We have attended the reli-gious ceremonies of each other's religions, so we have a basic understanding of the principles for which each religion stands, but it's been hard—I won't lie. There have been lots of tears and heated discus-sions, but we finally learned that compromise is the key. If you can't compromise in an interfaith relationship, it will never work.*
>
> TEREZ, NEW YORK

Finally, it came down to this: we both agreed before we got mar-ried that we wanted one religion for our family in which we would raise any future children. We didn't want to find a new religion to start from square one with or that was somewhere in the middle of both orthodoxies—an option a Catholic-Episcopal couple we know found in the Unitarian church—so it was either Judaism or Catholicism. Whichever of these religions we chose, we would immerse ourselves in it fully—participating in religious ceremonies when our children were born, attending church or temple on a weekly basis, and sending our children for religious instruction once they were old enough to qualify.

If we chose to go with Judaism, it would be my primary responsibility to educate Bill on the religion, its traditions, and rituals. If we went with Catholicism, all of that would be Bill's job. Once we reached this point, we each took some time to think about what lay ahead and to which degree we would be willing to commit to our respective religions. After a few days of thought, I was the one who came back to the discussion with my decision. I realized that I just didn't have it in me to create, maintain, and run a Jewish household. If we were going to do it, we would do it right—kosher home, lighting Sabbath candles, the works—and I just wasn't up for that. At the same time, I was comfortable with the notion of my children becoming Catholic and doing all that is required of that religion—being baptized, taking communion, and going to church. My decision was a great relief for Bill. It allowed him to fall back on the religion he knew the best and with which he felt most comfortable.

TEST YOUR DEVOTION TO FAITH

It may seem rather obvious that a couple coming into a marriage from two different religious backgrounds need to talk up front about their religious expectations, as Bill and I did, but the truth is, any couple getting married should really tackle this topic. We have friends who were brought up Catholic, married in a Catholic church, but have yet to baptize their school-age son. Recently, the wife was forced to join the local Catholic parish because she was going to be participating in a baptism as a godmother and needed written proof of her commitment to the Catholic community. It was this experience that finally got this couple talking about their spiritual future together as a family—some ten years after they were married and five years after their son was born—and now they're well on their way to planning a road map for their religious life together. Although they probably should have had this discussion years ago, some things are better late than never.

If you are marrying someone with a different religious background or from a different denomination within the same faith—and you plan to have children in your marriage—then discussing your future family's religion up front is especially critical. "To think that everything having to do with religion will flow into place once you have a child is very naive," says Fran Greene, a New York social worker who runs counseling groups for interfaith couples.

Wedding Wisdom

My husband is Jewish, and I was raised Christian. Aside from celebrating Christmas, I'm not a devout Christian. However, Judaism played a significant role in my husband's childhood and family life. It was clear how important it is to him to have our children raised Jewish, and we've also discussed my conversion, which I'll need to consider when we start our family. Thankfully, we think very much alike and agreed that conversion wouldn't be appropriate for purposes related to the wedding. Our family members are very accepting about our wishes and our decisions, which has also helped a lot.

CHANA, MASSACHUSETTS

To help you come to the spiritual decision that's right for your family, I've put together a set of questions that will test your devotion to your faith. I'm not saying that you have to become a church-going, Bible-thumping convert to whatever faith you choose, but before you become husband and wife, and especially before you bring any children into this world, you should have a clear sense of your relationship with God, how you feel about your faith (or your fiancé's faith, if it differs from yours), and what role religion will play in your family.

> ### Wedding Wisdom
> We agreed that because I felt so strongly about my faith, our children would be Roman Catholic and I would be responsible for the bulk of their religious education.
>
> SARAH, ILLINOIS

As you search for answers to the following ten questions, you'll get a better sense of your devotion (or lack thereof) to your faith, and it will help you determine what role religion will play in your life together. Granted, many of these questions are skewed toward a couple with differing religious backgrounds who are getting married, and some deal with outside factors, such as where you live or what kind of family you have; nonetheless, couples should go over each of these questions together.

Please remember this: there are no right or wrong answers to any of these questions. This exercise is simply designed to start a dialogue on religion between the two of you.

1. *Is one of you more devout than the other?* This question is applicable in all religious scenarios: two people of the same religion who are getting married or two people who come from differing religious backgrounds. The answer may be as obvious as which of you attends religious services at a church, synagogue, or mosque on a regular basis or as hidden as figuring out how much the faith you were raised in means to each of you and how that faith affects you

on a regular basis. For example, you may silently say a prayer before each meal or turn to quiet reflection or a religious ritual, such as counting rosary beads, when times are tough. Both are signs of a strong spiritual sense, and those need to be recognized when you're making any religious decisions for your future.

2. *Does your religion affect your everyday life in one way or another?* There are certain constants in some religions that go without question—and it's clear that they must continue to be a part of your life after you're married. These might include an Islamic man who prays a certain number of times a day—and who would need a place in his new home with his wife to continue this practice—or a Jewish woman who keeps a kosher home and doesn't eat dairy and meat products together. Therefore, she would have certain household requirements, such as separate sets of dishes, that would be absolutes in her mind.

3. *Are you uncomfortable with the notion of being religious, or does your fiancé's religion give you the willies—or vice versa?* I know a Jewish man who recently married a Catholic woman. They had "the talk" and decided that he was much more devoted to Judaism than she would ever be to Catholicism, and so they chose Judaism for their family's religion. Last year, they had their first son, and within hours of their son's birth, the husband started preparing for the *bris*, a religious ceremony that involves the cutting of a baby boy's foreskin. Although his wife knew that a *bris* was a big deal in the Jewish faith, she couldn't stomach the thought of it. To her, the *bris* felt like a televised torturing of her son. Never before had

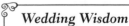

Wedding Wisdom
I cannot agree with my fiancé's Mormon beliefs, and we often get extremely angry when discussing faith (I'm Presbyterian). I have to admit we have not solved this issue yet, but plan to go to premarital counseling to help address it.

Jennifer, Texas

she voiced to her husband her concerns about the ceremony—because they hadn't thought to cover that territory. Now, here she was, just days away from the event that would symbolically welcome her son into the Jewish community, and all she could think about doing was paging her obstetrician and asking him to circumcise her son in the hospital so she wouldn't have to deal with the whole *bris* thing. Luckily, she expressed her feelings to her husband and didn't sneak a foreskin snipping behind his back. In response he assured her that they would get a topical anesthetic and apply it to their son's penis before the *bris* was to begin, which they did. Much to this woman's relief, her son slept through the event.

4. *Can you picture life without your current religion?* Obviously, this question is more appropriate for a couple who come from different religious backgrounds and who are grappling with which of their respective religions they'll choose for their family. When considering what life would be like without the Jewish faith, it wasn't hard for me to fathom: I'd pretty much stopped being a practicing Jew at age thirteen, or right after I celebrated my bat mitzvah. On the other hand, Bill had continued attending church right through the college years and into his twenties, when he became active in his parish. It was easy for us to answer this question: yes, I could picture life without my religion—and I was perfectly fine with that; no, Bill couldn't imagine life without Catholicism. "In my groups, it is usually the religion of the person who is more religious that the couple goes with for their family," says Greene.

5. *Is there a historical reason for choosing one religion over another?* If members of your family were persecuted for their religious beliefs in recent history, you may want to stick with or make your religion a focal point of your life, no matter what. The two examples that

come to mind, but that are surely not the only instances, are Jewish families with roots in World War II–era Europe and, most recently, Muslim families that hail from the Balkans. In these instances, different groups made a conscious effort to annihilate whole groups of people based on their religion and led to the Holocaust and "ethnic cleansing." I know a New York woman who was raised Jewish and whose grandparents on both sides were Holocaust survivors. Her grandparents had made it safely to American soil, but many of their siblings perished in concentration camps. To this woman, who was marrying a Methodist man, carrying on the Jewish heritage was her top priority. And although it wasn't in the cards for her to marry a Jewish man, at least she was marrying a man who was willing to let her religion take center stage in their family.

6. *Based on where you live, will practicing your religion be easy, enjoyable, and possible?* A couple raised as Mormon (also known as the Church of Jesus Christ of Latter-day Saints) would have no problem practicing their faith in Utah. But transplant that couple to somewhere else in the country where other religions dominate, and finding a house of worship or a sense of community may be challenging. That's not to say that one should put religion on a shelf because geography makes it inconvenient. Rather, if one or both of you were raised in a faith that is not prominent where you currently live yet you've made a respectable attempt at worship and have managed to find your own piece of religious community there, no matter how small, then I'd say that your diligence and commitment is a very strong sign of a tremendous devotion to your faith.

7. *How strong is your faith's lineage within your family?* Again, I'm going to use my husband and me as an example. When you look at the lineage of our faith, it's easy to see how we made the choice that we did. That's because even though Bill's cultural heritage is both German and Italian (although Italian is more dominant), the one constant throughout is Catholicism, which goes back generations in his family. In my family, there's more of a mix of religions, thus diluting my commitment to Judaism.

8. *Will either of your families put undue pressure on you when it comes to religion?* You may bristle at the thought of choosing your religion based on which family will put up the biggest stink, but you've got to live with your family—and only you know how miserable yours can make you. So, if you think your family will make an issue out of your religious choice, keep them in mind as you weigh your spiritual pros and cons.

9. *If you are giving up your religion, is there family nearby with whom you can celebrate certain holidays?* When I talk about giving up your religion, I realize that short of converting, you will never wholly give up your original religion. You're just choosing not to practice it on a regular basis. If you choose your fiancé's religion for your family and want your children to have a small sense of your religious identity, or if it will simply make you feel better to partake of certain religious celebrations on occasion, look to nearby family to help you accommodate this need. If there isn't family nearby to provide this sense of comfort and community, will you feel comfortable doing without your religion?

10. *Are you aware that the choice not to practice any religions is itself a religious decision?* I can't help but think of the 1980s band Rush and their song "Free Will," which had the following lyrics: "If you choose not to decide / you still have made a choice." The same is

true as you consider your religious devotion: if you decide not to choose a religion for your new family, then you have, in essence, made a choice. I would strongly advise against your going the avoidance route and ask that you remember my friend, whom I referenced in the beginning of the chapter. Because her parents did not choose a religion for their family and planned on leaving the religion decision up to her, what they did by proxy is choose nothing for her, and that's what she became: nothing. Now, whether or not you had a positive experience growing up in your respective religions, do you really want your children growing up and identifying their religion as "nothing"? If you can't decide which of your religions you want for your new family, at least find something that both of you can live with and that you can bring your children up within. Whether you attend Quaker meetings or give Buddhism a go, you

---

Wedding Wisdom

We certainly had to deal with the major issue of religion during our engagement. I am a practicing Roman Catholic, and my fiancé comes from a long line of Episcopal priests, including his own father, who definitely had the hardest time dealing with the issue of my faith and the faith of our potential children. At first my future father-in-law was very short with me, but I would not give up. I finally wrote him a letter about how much I loved his son, and continued to make a point of including him in our religious conversations whenever possible. Eventually he began to see that he could like me for the person I was, and get over the fact that I was Roman Catholic. It's not perfect yet, but it is improving.

SARAH, ILLINOIS

and your future children will find a sense of belonging in a spiritual community, so try to find one that works for all of you.

There are two final points I'd like to make, as far as devotion to faith goes. As I mentioned earlier, the ten questions here are designed simply to get a dialogue going on religion. If answering and talking about these questions helps you to come to a religion decision, great. But if they don't, don't give up. Rather, call in a professional—a counselor or spiritual leader who can help you work through some of the issues you may be facing. If you go the spiritual leader route, you may feel most comfortable seeking out someone affiliated with your faith, but buyer beware: interfaith couples may have trouble turning toward the clergy for guidance. "Clergy has their purpose in promoting their religion," says Greene, so an interfaith couple who approach a rabbi or priest for counseling may encounter resistance about their choice in who they're going to marry and possibly pressure for one of them to convert.

Finally, if you are in an interfaith or interdenominational relationship, when you finally arrive at the chosen religion for your family, understand that for the partner whose religion will not be included, there will be a grieving process. (This may be true for both of you if you choose a third religion for your family—say raising your children in the Episcopal Church when one of you is Catholic and the other is Jewish.) This process is completely normal, and you or your partner should expect to feel a loss on some level. You may also need to seek counseling or spiritual guidance to help you deal with the idea that a piece of one of your family's religious heritage will not be moving on into the next generation—your children. Be patient, kind, loving, and understanding with one another as you go through this transition, as it will only benefit and strengthen your family bond in the end.

BALANCING TWO RELIGIONS UNDER ONE ROOF

Although I've made it pretty clear in this chapter that I believe a family should have only one religion, I realize that there are situations where that simply won't fly. Perhaps you've just finished discussing your devotion to faith, thanks to the ten questions in this chapter, and you've determined that you're equally devoted to your faiths. In addition, neither of you is willing to give up your own religion, but you each want religion to be a part of your life. So, where does that leave you? Charting your own course on how you can make two religions work under one roof.

Before we get into some specifics on making it work, though, I wanted to point something out: when it comes to houses of worship, it is almost impossible to find one where you'll find two religions practiced, although the Unitarian Universalist Church comes closest in trying. This extreme left religious order openly welcomes people of all faiths and attempts to preach a spiritual message that is comforting and comfortable to all. But for the most part, if you and your fiancé are looking for a place to worship together—and the Unitarian Universalist method doesn't work for you—you're going to have to come to terms with the fact that you will have to attend a house of worship (synagogue, mosque, or church) where one religion takes precedence over another. Again, even though the Unitarian Universalist Church does a fine job of being open-minded about its congregation, it is a church, so a non-Christian partner may have some difficulty in dealing with the idea of going to a church to worship. Likewise, many Reform Jewish congregations have gone to great lengths to make Christians, Muslims, and spouses of other religions feel comfortable within their walls. This includes limiting portions of the service that are read in Hebrew and wel-

Interfaith Resources

I could write an entire book on what it takes to live a truly interfaith marriage, but that's not what this book is about. Although that topic is a small yet important part of *The Balanced Bride*, I suggest that you do further reading on the topic. Two recommended tomes on interfaith marriages are *Celebrating Our Differences: Living Two Faiths in One Marriage*, by Mary Rosenbaum (White Mane Publishing, 1999), and *The Interfaith Family Guidebook: Practical Advice for Jewish and Christian Partners*, by Joan C. Hawxhurst (Dovetail Publishing, 1998).

In addition, two organizations specialize in helping interfaith couples deal with the unique dynamics of their relationships. One is the Jewish Outreach Institute, which is geared more toward an interfaith family where Judaism is the primary religion. This group offers a list of synagogues across the country that welcome interfaith families. Check them out on the Web at joi.org.

The other is a secular organization called The Dovetail Institute for Interfaith Family Resources. (Its publishing arm put out the previously mentioned *Interfaith Family Guidebook*.) It offers advice and support for interfaith families, including an eponymous newsletter called *Dovetail,* which is by and for Christian and Jewish families. For more information on Dovetail, log on to dovetailpublishing.com or call 800-530-1596.

coming non-Jewish congregations' members to participate in the temple service. But the fact remains that you will be attending services at a synagogue each week, so the non-Jewish person in the family will have to grow comfortable with this scenario.

As you well know, a relationship is all about compromise, and this notion becomes even more important when you're dealing with a family of two religions. That's why I believe if you're going to make having two religions under one roof work, you will have to compromise or learn to live with the following four notions:

1. *Accept the placement of your partner's religious symbols in your home and vice versa.* Greene recalls counseling a Jewish-Catholic couple who were moving in together a few months before their wedding. After they'd unpacked the boxes, the man started nailing a cross into the wall above the couple's bed, and, as Greene put it, "the Jewish partner freaked out." Although the couple had talked intellectually about how they would balance both of their religions in their new family, they hadn't thought about the day-to-day details of living with a person of a differing religion. To the man, having a cross above his bed was a given, because that's how it had always been, ever since he was a kid. However, they hadn't broached the topic of how this would make her feel or, likewise, how he would feel when his Jewish partner lit candles on Friday night. A good way to come to terms with the presence of each other's religion's symbols is to talk about why they are important to each of you or, conversely, why they may make you feel uncomfortable. Together, you'll need to figure out how you can live with physical representations of each other's religion.

2. *By raising your children in both religions, you will have to forgo certain religious rites of passage that may have been a part of your*

own childhood. These rites of passage may start as early as when your child is born and you choose not to baptize your baby or have your son participate in a *bris.* The issue will come up again during the school years, when many children begin formal religious instruction and bring some of that instruction to fruition with first communion, confirmation, or a bar or bat mitzvah. On the other hand, although you may feel OK with your child forgoing these rites of passage, you should leave the topic open for discussion. That's because preteen or teenage children may begin to feel some sort of self-induced peer pressure from their friends who are experiencing certain religious affirmations, and suddenly your daughter may want to study Catholicism and get confirmed or your son may take an intense interest in Judaism and ask to prepare for a bar mitzvah. I suggest encouraging and supporting these interests, if and when your children express them.

3. *Make your religious parenting a team effort.* If you're going to raise your children with knowledge of both your religions, then you need to do it together. Don't make one Mom's religion and the other Dad's religion. Immerse yourself in each other's religion and learn all you can so that you can present a united front to your children. Additionally, you may want to consider joining two houses of worship. Yes, this will make for busy weekends of attending services at both places, but your children will experience both of your religions firsthand.

4. *Seek out support in the interfaith community.* Although it is surely challenging to come to grips with the idea of having an interfaith household, you don't have to go it alone—nor should you. There are literally millions of interfaith couples in America today, with about one million of them being a Christian-Jewish combination. You can

learn valuable negotiating tools and ways of working things out from the other couples who are going through exactly what you are — figuring out how to make a mixed marriage work. So, look on the Web, ask your local clergy to refer you to any local interfaith support groups, or research other interfaith resources (such as those suggested in the "Interfaith Resources" sidebar).

BALANCE: THE BOTTOM LINE

There are so many religious "mixed marriages" today that, should you and your fiancé grapple with which religion to practice in your future family, you should realize you're not going it alone. My husband and I are one of nearly one million marriages where one partner is Christian and the other is Jewish. That's not the only religious combination; I know plenty of Lutheran-Catholic, Methodist-Episcopalian, and Muslim-Christian families as well. But what many of us have in common is this: we chose one religion for our family instead of trying to balance two religions under one roof.

To decide exactly how you're going to handle the issue of religion in your future family, I've suggested that you test your devotion to faith. This chapter has provided ten thoughtful questions to consider as you test your individual devotion to faith. Then, hopefully, you'll be closer to your religion solution than when you started.

If you decide to go with both of your religions, I've provided resources for interfaith families. These are designed to help you learn how to balance two religions under one roof now and in the future, when you may add children to the picture.

11

MAKING YOUR CEREMONY MATTER

IN THE PREVIOUS chapter I talked extensively about why taking time today to figure out the role religion will play in your family tomorrow is imperative to your overall happiness. Now we need to talk about how those religious decisions are going to play out at your wedding and what level of spirituality your ceremony will have. This is especially tricky territory if one of you has a clear-cut idea of what you want for your wedding ceremony, and the other person's ideas are polar opposites. If you were raised in separate religions and can't figure out if you want both of your religions to be represented at your wedding, you'll need to talk about that as well.

Sometimes spirituality in a wedding has nothing to do with religion but rather the presence and participation of loved ones in the wedding ceremony. As with most things in marriage, you've got to communicate your feelings and your thoughts about how your ceremony will play out. Then you need to figure out a compromise that feels fair to both of you. Let me tell you a little about how one couple eventually figured out the form and substance of their wedding ceremony.

Like many of the East Coast couples I know, Brenda and Larry were raised in different religions. She's Catholic and he's Jewish. When they fell in love and decided to get married, their first thought was to have a religious wedding with both of their faiths represented. However, Brenda was divorced, and because she hadn't paid to have her first marriage annulled, she couldn't marry Larry in the Catholic Church. They didn't have much luck with Larry's religion either: many rabbis are concerned about the intermarrying of Jewish people, and they refuse to participate in or officiate at the wedding of a Jewish person marrying someone of a different religion. Brenda and Larry's wedding was to be no different.

> ### Wedding Wisdom
> We originally went to the rabbi at my in-laws' temple to see if she would officiate at our wedding, but she refused because I'm Christian. We asked friends we know who have interfaith marriages if they could recommend a rabbi. We finally found one who ended up doing an eloquent and touching service.
>
> SHANNON, VERMONT

The couple's difficulty in finding a religious figure to marry them got them talking about what life would be like after marriage, and, considering how both the Catholic Church and the Jewish faith looked upon their union, they figured that they didn't want to worship in either religion. So, they looked for some common ground, and although both found some comfort in the Episcopal Church, they weren't sure if that was the right place for them to get married. They met with the church's pastor to talk about what kind of wedding ceremony they might have, should they be married there. They liked many elements of the ceremony that the pastor proposed—it had some of the orthodoxy of Catholicism but felt comfortable to Larry as well. But in the end

Brenda and Larry decided to have a civil ceremony. They figured that a great way to bring an element of spirituality to their wedding ceremony without choosing one religion over another would be to have friends and family do readings from the Bible and sing certain songs, which is what they did. What they ended up with was a well-balanced ceremony that had a touch of Catholicism here and a dab of Judaism there but that also felt right to both Brenda and Larry.

Choosing Your Ceremony

Regardless of whether you're marrying someone of the same religion or a differing religion, what is important about Brenda and Larry's story is it shows how circuitous planning your wedding ceremony can be—and should be. Your wedding day is one of the most important days in your life—it is the day you become husband and wife—and so you shouldn't just go with a cookie-cutter ceremony that all your friends have had or that your spiritual leader suggests. For your wedding ceremony to be meaningful for you and for those

Wedding Wisdom

Although I was raised Presbyterian, I started attending my husband's Catholic church when we were dating. We both liked the parish and the priest and decided to have our wedding there when we got engaged. We wanted the ceremony to be meaningful for my Protestant family even though it took place in a Catholic church. We decided to ask the minister from my church back home, who is also a good friend of the family, to be part of the ceremony by doing New and Old Testament readings.

CORI, ILLINOIS

involved, it should reflect who you are as a couple, what you believe in, and what you hope to communicate to those who will witness your union.

One of the first places to start in your search for the spiritual level of your ceremony is with the person who will marry you. Of course, two people with the same religious background who want to be married in a religious ceremony have it the easiest: you just go with what you know. Now, if you face a situation like Brenda and Larry did, where going with a religious figure from either religion is out of the question, you'll need to do some soul-searching while searching for an officiant.

Some people feel that if they are married anywhere but a house of worship, God won't be present and therefore their marriage won't feel "real." If this is how you feel, then limit your search to clergy only. Others have "left" their original religion and would feel hypocritical being married with any element of that religion present. So, for them, an extremely liberal clergyman or -woman might be their best bet, such as one from the Unitarian Church or Ethical Culture Society (a spiritual society that is people-centered, rather than faith-based). Or they may simply want to go with a civil ceremony, if that's a marriage option in your state (not all states recognize civil marriages).

> **Wedding Wisdom**
>
> *I am Catholic; my husband's family is Buddhist. Neither of us is particularly religious, but my immediate family is. I did not want to put my fiancé through pre-cana in the Catholic tradition, and we wanted to get married at an outside venue. So I called up a family friend who is a reverend at a Unitarian Church. He was more than happy to marry us.*
>
> SARA, NEW YORK

The most important thing to keep in mind once you've identified the kind of officiant you want at your wedding is that this officiant should work with you to craft a wedding ceremony that feels personal to you, not what he or she thinks is the perfect wedding ceremony. Conversations with your officiant that include "you must do this" or "we should do that" are red flags in my book. I'd rather see your officiant saying things like "Well, we could do this, but it's up to you." Of course, I feel the need to add a caveat to this statement: if you're going to be married in a house of worship, you must respect the rules of the place. So, if your officiant's suggestions keep your ceremony in line with the house of worship's standard practices, then you must show deference to them. For example, let's say that you want to have a Catholic mass for your wedding ceremony and you tell the priest who will be officiating that you want everyone in the audience to take part in communion. Well, chances are he's not going to go along with that, especially if all of your invited guests aren't Catholic, because that request isn't keeping in line with Catholic rituals. However, if you are getting married in the Episcopal Church, where communion is open to any parishioner, the pastor would probably agree to your request without any hesitation.

Wedding Wisdom

For the wedding we used the traditional Jewish wedding canopy (chuppah) and Jewish marriage contract (ketubah). It was really special to pick out our ketubah, which describes our personal vows to each other. My husband took on the project of building our chuppah (rather than borrowing or renting one). I came home one night from work to see the finished product in our living room! For the actual canopy, we used Jewish prayer shawls (tallit) belonging to Mike's father, his grandfathers, and his great-grandfather. All of these items made the wedding so meaningful, and emphasized the closeness and importance of family.

CHANA, MASSACHUSETTS

Terry Barber is a United Methodist minister in St. Louis, Missouri. He has presided over hundreds of weddings of brides and grooms of various religions. Here, he talks about how he goes about crafting a spiritual and meaningful wedding ceremony for couples.

The most important thing for me is that the ceremony reflect the couple's spirituality and their own beliefs. The wedding should be a time when people are making a commitment to each other in front of their creator or God or their maker, or however they define a higher being, plus the people who are closest to them.

I usually start with what I call a "skeleton ceremony," which is a pretty liberal, open ceremony. There is some spirituality to it, so that people of most religions will feel comfortable with it. For example, it includes the Lord's Prayer. I tell the couple that we can say the prayer or sing it, whichever they prefer. Or, for those who say, "Well, I don't believe in the Trinity," we can take it out. I think the worst thing that you can do

---

Wedding Wisdom

My fiancé is Catholic and I am Jewish, so from the beginning of our relationship we had issues with discussing religion. To put another layer on top of this, his father is Palestinian, his mother is of German descent (and Catholic), I was born in Israel, and my parents are very spiritually Jewish. Sometimes it was hard to watch the news together, but my fiancé and I have developed an awareness and appreciation of both religions and cultures. We are incorporating a couple of prayers from each religion, but we're basically having a nondenominational ceremony.

TEREZ, NEW YORK

during a wedding ceremony is to have people come together and say vows or words that mean nothing to them. I don't care if they were raised Protestant, Catholic, or Jewish, I don't think it's a good idea to have hypocrisy in the ceremony.

To get a better sense of how religious their ceremony should be, I usually start by asking, "What are your religious backgrounds like?" and "How religious would you say you are?" If I find out that one of the members is either Catholic or Jewish and can't be married in his or her house of worship because of divorce or doesn't want to be but would still like to have that faith represented, I'll try to do whatever he or she likes. I've had weddings with Catholic priests and rabbis involved, where they would say a prayer or a blessing. At other times, I might be marrying a Catholic couple who don't want a priest there but still want the ceremony to "feel" Catholic. So, I'll make sure that the ceremony involves candle lighting and that I wear a robe. That way it looks and feels like a religious ceremony. The robe says to the people in the audience, "Ah, this is an ordained person," and that means a lot to the family. In addition, it means a lot to the couple because it shows them that I'm not just an ordained Methodist minister but also a minister who is willing to go their way and make their wedding ceremony more meaningful for them and their families.

As far as the ceremony itself goes, I always try to make what I'm saying or talking about reach people on a deeper level. So, if the couple say that they want to include a reading from First Corinthians, one of the most popular wedding selections, I'll let them know that not only will we read that passage, but then I'm going to paraphrase it as I walk down into the audience. I'll say something like, "What that reading actually means is that love keeps no score of wrongs," and I might even ask, "Did everyone hear that?" I find that brings the audience into the whole wedding ceremony more and makes it more moving than if I just stood up there and read that passage.

I also let my couples know that some of the most moving ceremonies I've ever attended or presided over were those where family members or friends got involved, so that is something for them to consider. It could be as simple as having the ceremony include a vows recital that includes the audience or as elaborate as asking members of the family to write something personal that they'll read. There was one wedding where a father got up to say something to his daughter—not a toast really but more a testimonial of his love for his daughter. It took a lot of guts for that man to say that in front of the audience, and those things are hard to beat. At another wedding, the groom wanted to sing a solo to his bride and the bride read a poem to the groom, but both became so choked up that I read both passages. And even though I ended up reading them, because they were from the bride and groom to each other, they touched us all on a higher level.

The reason I like to involve family and friends is this: the church will always be there for this couple, but the first time they have a crisis and they need someone to talk to, chances are they won't turn to their priest at first. They'll look to their family and friends for support. So, if they can involve those special people in their ceremony, that draws them all closer together in the long run.

> **Wedding Wisdom**
>
> *Originally we wanted a rabbi and a priest to officiate, but when that was not to be, we found an "interfaith minister" on the Internet who has a deep knowledge of both religions. We're writing our ceremony from start to finish with him.*
>
> TEREZ, NEW YORK

WRITING YOUR OWN VOWS

One of the ways to make a ceremony meaningful is to have a hand in the vows you'll recite. Many of the couples that Barber marries request to do this, and he's comfortable doing so, but with some guidelines. "I tell them that in a vacuum, writing your own vows seems like a great thing to do, but when you actually sit down to write them, it's harder than you think," he says. "Either they end up not knowing what to say or writing too much. I mean, there are only so many ways that you can say, 'I love you' to someone." Sometimes couples forge ahead undeterred in writing their vows but without great success. "I always give the couple a deadline, because I want to see those vows before the actual ceremony. So, the wedding is seven months away, and I'll keep asking and asking to see the vows, and then finally two weeks before the wedding, they'll say, 'Well, let's just go with what you have.'"

Or instead of procrastinators, Barber will have to deal with a jumble of words or something that is inappropriate for a wedding ceremony. "The couple may have read a bunch of books and put pieces together. Or they have a phrase here and there that they

---

Wedding Wisdom

My fiancé is a lapsed Jew, while I am a lapsed Protestant. Yet both of us like the traditions of our religions and we go to church or temple when we feel the need. What are we doing for our ceremony? We found a husband and wife team—he is a rabbi and she is a reverend. We're working with them to write our own ceremony and to intertwine elements of Judaism and Christianity (you'd be surprised at the similarities). We're both very happy, as are our families.

MELISSA, NEW YORK

might say in privacy but that wouldn't be right in front of 250 people," he says. "So what you end up with is a fragmented ceremony,
which I then help them to refine."

Vow Writing Simplified

If you're inspired to take a stab at writing your own vows,
here are some additional pointers to keep in mind:

- *Keep it simple.* Instead of paraphrasing all of your favorite
  love songs or passages from great books, choose one,
  maybe two elements of either and use them as a small part
  of the ceremony. One or two minutes of sentimental prose
  will mean more to each other and your audience than a
  passage that seems to drag on forever.

- *Do it as a team effort.* If only one of you is comfortable with
  writing vows, then you'll need to compromise to both take
  a stab at adding some personal words or to not write your
  vows at all. On the other hand, this is one of the most
  important days of your lives, and you will want a ceremony
  that followed your hearts, not someone else's rules. If one
  of you wants to do a recitation, do it. The other can
  "answer" with a song sung or played by a professional
  musician.

- *Read the vows you write out loud.* As a writer, I've learned
  that reading my work aloud is critical to having smooth-

Although Barber supports his couples in looking for ways to personalize their wedding ceremony—and the officiant you choose should, too—when it comes to vows, he encourages them to stick

sounding prose. Sometimes words on paper *look* right, but when you read them out loud, they simply don't *sound* right. Before the ceremony, read them out loud to a friend or family member, who might pick up on some kinks in your craft that you missed.

- *Practice your prose.* Once you've settled on the vows you'll use, practice saying them. This allows you to really think about what you're saying and to become comfortable with the flow of the words.

- *Memorization is unnecessary.* Although practice may make perfect, attempting to memorize your vows will put undue pressure on you. You have no idea how nervous you'll feel once you get up in front of your audience, and even remembering your fiancé's name may be a feat of Herculean effort! Instead, give your officiant your scripted vows, have him or her read them first, and then you repeat them. Your officiant may wear a microphone, so whatever he or she says will be audible to everyone. But what you say to each other will be heard by only you and your officiant. So, even if you mess up, people probably won't even be aware of it.

with the tried-and-true. "I tell them to take the basic vows," he says, "and then do a variation on a theme."

BLENDING RELIGIONS, TRADITIONS, AND RITUALS

As a Catholic man and a Jewish woman, my husband and I faced many challenges in planning a wedding that would reflect both of our religious heritages without offending anyone in the process. Although we ended up going with a civil ceremony, if I could do it all over again, I probably would have worked harder to find the similarities in our faiths and incorporate them in our ceremony somehow. But at the time of our wedding, I hadn't invested in learning about Catholicism nor had Bill studied up on Judaism, so we were working from a position of ignorance rather than knowledge. Now, many years later and after attending countless masses with my husband and children, I can see so many parallels between Catholic and Jewish rituals and how those similarities would have been beautiful to use in our ceremony. For example, both religions include blessings of bread and wine. Additionally, both use candle lighting. And music and song play a key part in both religious services as well.

I realize that I've simplified the similarities, but it's hard to deny their existence. So, if you're marrying someone of a different faith and are looking to blend traditions and rituals from each of your faiths, do what I *didn't*: look for the similarities among the faiths and figure out ways to work them into your ceremony. If you're a Catholic-Jewish couple, see if you can get a priest and a rabbi to participate, with the priest saying the blessing of the Eucharist and the rabbi reciting the blessing in Hebrew for the bread and wine. For an added personal touch, invest in a pewter or silver goblet that you can use in the wedding ceremony as both a chalice and kiddush cup; that cup will become a family keepsake because it was part of your wedding.

Another way to add a touch of the Jewish faith to a ceremony is to be married under a *chuppah,* or a wedding canopy. This canopy is held together by four poles, which members of the wedding party may hold or which might be secured to the ground. The *chuppah* is supposed to represent the home that the bride and groom will make together once they're married, and, like a marriage, the *chuppah* is fragile and can fall down at any moment.

Sometimes, blending traditions and rituals at your wedding is more of a nod to your cultural background than your religions per se. For example, I've attended a number of weddings where the bride of Asian descent chose a bright red wedding dress over a traditionally white one. (Asian cultures see white as the color of death and red as the color of happiness.) Likewise, if the bride or groom is of African-American descent, she or he may want to add the jumping of the broom to the wedding ceremony.

> **Wedding Wisdom**
>
> *What saved the day for us—I'm Catholic and my husband is Protestant—was when a friend of my husband's family, a Baptist minister, said he would perform the ceremony. I'm glad we got married in a church. It met the approval of our parents and any religious relatives. For us it symbolized heritage, family, and community, and became a more formal ritual than a quick "I do," which the civil ceremony we were considering would have been.*
>
> HEATHER, MASSACHUSETTS

Other traditions to consider adding to create an inclusive ceremony follow:

- *Wear certain clothing.* Earlier in this chapter, Barber talked about how he'll don a robe when presiding over a wedding where one or both of the people are of the Catholic faith. Well, the clergy of many other religions also wear robes during services, including those at Episcopal churches and Jewish temples. So, if you want your officiant to reflect your heritage in how he or she dresses, request that he or she wear a robe. In addition, you may extend the idea of dressing a certain way to your invited guests. For example, if you're planning to have elements of a Jewish ceremony in your wedding, hand out *yarmulkes,* or Jewish head coverings, to the men in the audience. If your husband's family hails from a culture where men or women dress a certain way for celebratory affairs, see if you can't work those elements into how you or your wedding party dress. One couple I know represented the following combination: a Lutheran woman marrying a Muslim man whose family hailed from the Persian Gulf area. There, men customarily wear elaborate swords at weddings, and so this man wore one with his traditional suit at their nondenominational ceremony.

Wedding Wisdom

I am of Irish ancestry and my husband is Chinese-American. The combination made for a colorful and fun ceremony—red and pink, as red is the traditional color for Chinese weddings. Our ceremony readings included one Chinese poem, read in English and Mandarin, as well as lyrics from a traditional Irish wedding song.

SARA, NEW YORK

• *Alter the processional.* To give a nod to Jewish ritual, have both parents walk the bride and groom down the aisle instead of just the father of the bride walking his daughter down the aisle.

• *Break a glass at the end of the ceremony.* This is a Jewish custom that some believe is supposed to represent the destruction of the long-ago temple in Jerusalem, a story that is part of the Old Testament. Others liken it to the fragility of a marriage, much like the *chuppah.* You can do a twist on the traditional by having both the bride and groom break the glass. (It is usually something the man does only.) I've heard of couples who choose glasses made of brightly colored glass, which they collect after breaking them and then use as a decorative item in their home, incorporated into a work of art, for example.

• *Light a Unity candle, which is a Christian tradition.* Barber likes to take the Unity candle one step further. Instead of lighting two candles into one and then making the one candle become the central focus of the lighting ceremony, he suggest keeping the two original candles lit for a total of three candles. "Yes, you're a couple and you're joining together to become a family," he says, "but you're still special and unique individuals within the relationship." If the bride and groom have children, he likes to involve those children in the candle lighting as well by having more candles represented.

> **Wedding Wisdom**
> *My husband and I had a traditional Indian wedding as we are both from India but raised in the United States.*
> SHARAYU, OREGON

• *Take communion.* This act is an important part of Catholic and other Christian churches' rituals. If one or both of you want to add this religious element to your ceremony, have a priest or pastor there to offer communion.

• *Sign a* ketubah, *or Jewish marriage license.* The *ketubah* originated as a contract to signify the transaction of the groom acquiring the bride as property. Thankfully, Jewish marriage licenses no longer include such arcane language. What has remained is the artistic quality of the *ketubah,* which features ornate Hebrew lettering and illustrative decorations. Many couples frame the *ketubah* and hang it in their bedroom.

BALANCE: THE BOTTOM LINE

Sometimes in the craziness that comes with planning a wedding, you forget the reason for your celebration: your fiancé and you are joining together to become husband and wife. While finding a caterer, deejay, and reception location are all important for your wedding-day bliss, what really matters most is the wedding ceremony—the time when you're actually getting married.

In this chapter I've offered ways that you can make your wedding ceremony matter to you. For example, find a location, such as a house of worship, and an officiant that together will best represent your faith and the meaning of the day to both of you. In addition, I believe you should craft a ceremony that reflects who you two are—as religious people, as people in love, and as the couple who want to become a family by becoming husband and wife. Finally, I've provided ideas on how you can weave in elements from your religious backgrounds and write your own vows. Taken together, these suggestions should help you craft a meaningful ceremony.

12

FORGING A
SPIRITUAL BOND

WHEN I WAS dating my husband, Bill, there was one defining moment when I realized that he was my soul mate. It came almost instantly after I had an epiphany that told me that we would get married, have children, and spend the rest of our lives together. I want to tell you a bit about how Bill and I became soul mates. Then, I want you to see if you can recognize any of the same or similar occurrences happening in your dating, courtship, and engagement. Why? Because I think it's critical for people who are marrying to be soul mates. Don't worry if you read through this chapter and don't see all the elements of your relationship with your fiancé. Even though I believe only soul mates should marry, I also believe that two people can grow to become soul mates over time. Now, let me tell you about the history of my relationship with my husband.

MY SOUL MATE

Before we became engaged, Bill and I had dated for about two years, in what was more of a friendship than a bona fide relationship. We'd known each other during high school and had reconnected after college, when we bumped into each other on a train platform. We'd both gone to visit our mothers in our hometown one weekend and were catching a train back to New York City.

After we ran into each other, we would occasionally do datelike things, like see a movie or go to dinner, but I never felt like we were truly dating. There was never any holding of hands or kissing good night. We were just two people with a similar past who liked to do things together.

Close to that fateful night when I realized Bill was my soul mate, I'd had another epiphany about my life: I'd realized I'd had enough of the dating scene and that I was ready to find someone to marry. I know that seems like an odd thing to declare, because potential husbands don't just show up on your doorstep every day, but making this life decision helped clarify my outlook when I met men and considered dating them.

Soon thereafter, I realized that Bill had the most husband potential of any man I was spending time with. Even though I'd known him since my teens, however, it dawned on me that I didn't actually know him that well, but I knew that I wanted to know him better. Problem was, whenever we got together, we always reminisced about our

> **Wedding Wisdom**
>
> *Our friends and family were aware that for most of the early relationship (we were college sweethearts), it was my husband who pursued me. However, what nobody knew until our wedding ceremony was that about a month into our relationship I wrote in my journal "I will marry Peter Goldberg," and dated it. I had this journal entry printed in the program to everyone's surprise — including Peter's!*
>
> ADELE, NEW YORK

school days. So, the next time we got together, I attempted to steer our conversations away from "Do you remember when . . ." and into the here and now. We talked about our work, living in New York City, and our families. It was wonderful getting to know someone I'd known for so long but actually knew very little about.

That evening, I discovered that Bill and I had a lot in common, besides our high school and hometown. Like my parents, his mother and father were divorced, and he'd had a hard time adjusting to it, just like I had. We talked about custody weekends and feeling torn between our mother and father, and that shared experience alone

The Lighter Side: Why Men Marry

The publishers of Harlequin romance novels (you know, those bodice-ripping books people love to hate yet actually read in private) recently surveyed men nationwide on when and why the spirit moves them to marry. Here's what some of them had to say:

- 44 percent marry "simply because he loves her."
- 15 percent get married "to find a life companion."
- 6 percent tie the knot "because they want to have children."
- 2 percent get betrothed as a way of getting into an exclusive relationship.
- 1 percent each said marriage was a way of getting out of the singles scene and a means to an end when finances were concerned.

made me feel a little bit closer to him. On our next date, we continued discussing shared experiences, this time delving into issues surrounding our own failed relationships and the career paths we each wanted to take. That night, we held hands for the first time as we walked back to my apartment. Then, I invited Bill in, something I'd never done before, and we sat on my couch and continued our talk. It was on that couch that I felt an unexplainably strong pull toward Bill—like a giant magnet connecting us—and all I wanted to do was hug him. So, I did. We sat together until three o'clock in the morning, doing nothing but holding each other and talking. It was at that moment I knew Bill was the right person for me. I know he felt the same way, too, because we got engaged a year later, and tied the knot shortly thereafter. Now we have two beautiful children, and, as I write this, we're edging up on our ten-year anniversary. I'm confident we will spend the rest of our lives as husband and wife.

Wedding Wisdom

One day I was visiting with a girlfriend from college. We were talking about the men in our lives, including the guy I was dating (now my husband). She asked what I liked most about Mike, and as I'm listing off things—"he's funny, smart, ambitious, responsible"—I realized that these were all the personality traits I'd ever wanted in "the one." I made a mental note about it, and six months later, he popped the question. How could I say no?

CHANA, MASSACHUSETTS

When I tell people now of that moment of knowing that Bill was my soul mate, I realize that I sound dramatic and very Hollywood, but it's how it happened. In a matter of minutes, I knew that I'd found my soul mate and best friend, and an incomplete part of my life was now complete. Bill and I had connected on a higher level; we'd forged a spiritual bond.

Even though I'm not a very religious person, I believe that some sort of force brought Bill and me together. I think about how fate reunited us—visiting our mothers on the same weekend and taking the same train back to New York City together. There were so many variables that could have prevented us from seeing each other on the train platform, but somehow we met and got together. I'd like to believe that somehow that meeting was orchestrated by something greater than us and that it was all meant to be. For that I'm very thankful.

Many other married women I've talked to have also had that sort of lightning-bolt moment or epiphany when they realized that their then-boyfriend was the one for them. Here is how Kelly, a writer in Chicago, experienced that moment.

"About three or four months into our relationship, which was long-distance dating, I was taking a shower, and I got a very clear message in my mind. Suddenly, I realized that my boyfriend Eric was a gift from God, and what I did with him was up to me," says Kelly. "Something like that has never happened to me before. I believe in God, and I pray, but I don't lead a so-called godly life. It was one of those things where, whoa, I don't know why it happened, but it made me realize that he was the person I was supposed to be with."

Kelly and Eric were married in 1997, and now they're trying to start a family.

ARE YOU SOUL MATES?

What is important in these two anecdotes is that both Kelly and I found ourselves being inexplicably drawn to our respective spouses and feeling as if a higher power had arranged it all. We'd found our soul mates, and each of us could pinpoint exactly when we knew we'd found them.

In my opinion, there are two key elements that help determine the long-term potential of a relationship. One, the partners involved must view each other as a "soul mate" and "best friend." And two, each person should feel a developing bond with the other person — a bond that makes you both feel as though your spirits mesh. That bond should include feelings of true friendship, a shared value system, and long-term views of life that run parallel with each other.

You may be wondering whether the two of you are already soul mates — or on your way to becoming them. As I mentioned before, I believe that only soul mates should marry — and that marrying your soul mate is one of life's greatest gifts. A marriage between soul mates is one that's built on a solid base and is likely to endure when other less-solid relationships crumble — especially in times of crisis. That's why I want you to determine where you and your fiancé score on the

Soul Mate Quiz

	Y	N
1. Did you have an epiphany or an "aha!" moment when you suddenly knew that you wanted to spend the rest of your life with your fiancé?	—	—
2. Can you already picture your fiancé fathering your children (if you want children)?	—	—
3. Were you nervous about getting intimate with your fiancé and/or have you decided to postpone intercourse until you're married?	—	—
4. Do you feel as if you've known your fiancé your whole life, even if you only met recently?	—	—
5. Have you discovered that your and your fiancé's paths crossed or almost crossed at some time during your life without your realizing it? Do you feel like they should have?	—	—

soul mate scale *before* you say, "I do." To that end, I've designed the "Soul Mate Quiz."

The ten questions in the "Soul Mate Quiz" won't take much time to complete, but I believe the quiz will provide you with great insight into your relationship. It's designed to help you uncover ways you two can work on ensuring that you do indeed become soul mates, if you aren't already, by the time you become Mr. and Mrs. You may discover that you became soul mates long ago but just didn't know it, and this quiz will be a wonderful reminder of how perfect the two of you are for each other.

Each question requires a yes or no answer. Then, once you've answered all the questions, read on for my analysis of your soul mate

	Y	N
6. Was meeting your fiancé dependent on a set of circumstances that, had one variable been changed, you might not have met? Does it seem like you were brought together by fate?	—	—
7. Do you often finish each other's sentences?	—	—
8. When you and your fiancé speak about such things in life as your values, do you feel as if you're speaking in one voice? When you disagree, do you maintain deep mutual respect for each other?	—	—
9. Have you ever predicted when your fiancé might call or what he may be thinking?	—	—
10. Is your fiancé your best friend?	—	—

status. Not everyone who takes this quiz will come up with a perfect soul mate score, and that's OK. I've provided ideas and exercises on how to strengthen your soul mate connection with your future spouse. By the time you walk down the aisle, I want you to feel confident that you are marrying not only the love of your life, but your soul mate, too.

Ideally, you will have answered yes to all ten questions. Doing so, I believe, is an excellent predictor of two people already at the point of being soul mates. But if some of your answers were no, don't worry. There's still time for you to forge a spiritual bond with your fiancé and become his soul mate.

Now, let's examine what each question represents in your relationship. Then read on for suggestions on what you can do or discussions you can have with your fiancé so that you can connect, become soul mates, and create and maintain a strong spiritual bond as a couple—and ultimately as a family.

> **Wedding Wisdom**
> *I knew he was the one when I couldn't imagine living my life without him. From the moment I met him, it was like slow motion in a movie, and I knew I couldn't live in this world without him being a part of my life. When I called my mother to tell her this, she said "I think you are going to marry this guy; you've never talked about anyone else like this before." She was right.*
>
> CAMERON, TEXAS

Question 1. Did you have an epiphany or an "aha!" moment when you suddenly knew that you wanted to spend the rest of your life with your fiancé?

Some of us are more in tune with our feelings than others, so you may have already had this relationship epiphany and not even realized it. Although it is not a prerequisite to marital bliss, many happily married couples can point to a moment in time when they suddenly knew that their

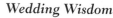

Wedding Wisdom

After we dated for over a year, I was offered the chance to spend five months in London, going to school and interning at a great British firm. It was then I realized that no matter how far apart we would be or how long it would be, I never wanted to let go of him. I went to live in London without him and, although I missed him terribly, it only made our relationship stronger. It's now been five wonderful years that he has been a part of my life, and from the moment I considered life without him, I knew how lucky I was to have found him and to have him in my life.

BONNIE, ILLINOIS

boyfriend or girlfriend was the person they wanted to spend the rest of their lives with. It's possible that this revelation may have come at an odd time, like it did when Kelly was taking a shower, or following an especially important or emotional time in your life. Think back on your courtship with your fiancé. Can you recall a time when a picture of the two of you twenty years in the future popped into your head? Or perhaps you once envisioned what your future children would look like. Or maybe your epiphany happened rather subtly. Perhaps one day you simply realized that of all the guys you've dated, this one made the most sense. It's a wonderful thing to experience true love, and having had this epiphany, however large or small, obvious or subtle, you're well on your way to forming a spiritual bond with your future husband.

Question 2. Can you already picture your fiancé fathering your children (if you want children)?

This is the one question on the "Soul Mate Quiz" when a no answer is just as acceptable as a yes one. That's because this question is designed to help you determine whether you've sufficiently broached the subject of having children—not to make you act as a fortune-teller and predict the birth order of your sons and daughters or what you'll name them. One of the most motivating factors for a man and woman to get married is to legally form a family and have children. If you have no idea where your fiancé stands on children—how many he wants, when he wants to start having them, or even if he wants them at all—then you two need to sit down and do some talking. It would be awfully sad for a couple to come together as a husband and wife and have one person expect to become a parent when the other person isn't interested in having children at all. Of course, as you begin to discuss children, you may realize that neither of you wants to have them. That's OK. The most important thing is that you are both on the same wavelength about starting (or not starting) a family.

Question 3. Were you nervous about getting intimate with your fiancé and/or have you decided to postpone intercourse until you're married?

A strange thing happens on the way to falling in love. You date a lot of people—and possibly become intimate with many of them. Often, that intimacy means nothing more than satisfying a physical need. Then, along comes the person you suspect you're going to marry, and suddenly you're as nervous as a high school student going to her first prom. Having sex is the furthest thing from your mind— or at least not the top of the list. You realize that you really want to get to know this person first, before you become intimate—whether that intimacy occurs during your courtship or after you're married. This may seem ironic, but I believe this feeling of slight trepidation is a good sign. It means that you've finally developed a relationship that has more significance than relationships you've had in the past.

With this man, it isn't just about sex. It's about being with someone who makes you truly happy, and when you're ready to become intimate, you will. But there's no reason to rush.

Question 4. Do you feel as if you've known your fiancé your whole life, even if you only met recently?

When you connect with another person on a higher level, you become closer than you've ever been to anyone else in your life. It's hard to imagine what life was like before that person became a part of your life, and in essence, the past somehow slips away. If you find yourself looking back on your life and saying, "Gosh, I can't even imagine what things were like before he was a part of my life," then you've made a big step into fully enveloping your fiancé into your life. The time when he wasn't around doesn't matter anymore. He's here now, he loves you, and you love him. That's what it's all about when it comes to being soul mates.

Question 5. Have you discovered that your and your fiancé's paths crossed or almost crossed at some time during your life but without your realizing it? Do you feel like they should have?

Friends of ours who live in Virginia have been happily married for more than ten years. My husband introduced them in high school, they dated throughout college, and then they married soon thereafter.

Wedding Wisdom

My husband and I met long distance and knew about each other for years before we actually met. That's because he's best friends with the husband of my college roommate, and from freshman year to senior year, she kept talking about her (then) boyfriend's friend and how I had to meet him. When I finally did, the year after we graduated college, I just knew I would end up marrying him—that he was the one I was supposed to be with. I was very comfortable and happy with him from the very start.

MELISSA, PENNSYLVANIA

They are still madly in love these many years later, and have two beautiful boys. But recently they discovered that they were in the same kindergarten class. During first grade, their hometown reorganized the school district, and they were forever in different schools. It was amazing for them to learn that they had been classmates many years ago, and they wonder whether that had something to do with their eventually coming together.

I know of another married couple whose paths almost crossed many times during their high school and college years, for instance, attending the same event or playing in the same park—but they never met until they took full-time jobs years later at the same airport. One fateful day, they bumped into each other, struck up a conversation, and eventually started dating. Today, they are happily married soul mates with a young son.

Sometimes it seems as though God or some other higher power acts like a marionette master, orchestrating lots of near misses with your soul mate until one day your paths eventually cross. What all of these close calls signify is the fact that your soul mate shares similarities with you, whether it be the town where he lives, the activities he enjoys, or the career he chose. Without these kinds of important similarities, you couldn't become soul mates.

If you can't find any of these so-called near-misses with your fiancé, sit down with him one night and review your respective road maps of life. I'm confident that in exploring your past, you'll find some common bond that somehow connects you in place and time.

Question 6. Was meeting your fiancé dependent on a set of circumstances that, had one variable been changed, you might not have met? Does it seem like you were brought together by fate?
This question really hits home for me. I often wonder: if I'd taken a different train back to New York City the weekend I met Bill or even

if I hadn't gone to visit my mother at all, would the two of us have ever come together on our own? I'll never know the answer to that question, but, like with question five, I'm a big believer in the notion that a force greater than us makes certain things happen in our lives. Think about the circumstances that led up to your meeting your fiancé. Could something have changed that would have prevented you from meeting? Do you ever wonder about that? Does it feel like fate played a part in your meeting your future husband? Let me tell you about a woman I know named Sandy who constantly marvels at all the circumstances that had to come together for her to meet her husband.

One weekend shortly after her five-year college reunion, Sandy visited her college friend Lisa in Lisa's hometown. One evening they

---

Wedding Wisdom

I met my husband, Richard, at a consulting job I had for six months. We had a friendly, easy way of working together, but when the project was over, we said our good-byes and that was that. (I was married at the time.) Three years later—and now divorced—I was in a restaurant having dinner with friends. Through the windows we saw someone ride up on one of my favorite motorcycles. We all laughed about the "knight in shining armor arriving on a MotoGuzzi" to meet me. When the knight came in and took off his helmet, it was Richard! I invited him to meet my friends. When I looked him in the eye and shook his hand, I knew something changed between us. He later told me that in his twelve years of dating after his divorce, he had never felt anything like "the freight train hitting him" as it did when he shook my hand. We knew in that moment that we would always be together.

SHARON, MICHIGAN

went out to see a band at a local club, and, at the last minute, Lisa invited another friend, Pam, who called her brother, Mike, to join them at the club. Mike, who normally works the night shift, was off that evening and almost missed his sister's call. Luckily, he picked up the receiver right when Pam was ready to hang up. Mike agreed to meet Pam and Lisa at the club, where they introduced him to Sandy. Mike and Sandy hit it off, began dating long distance, and eventually got married.

If you don't often think about everything that went into meeting your fiancé (like the way Mike and Sandy came together), you should—and you should be thankful for it. Had those circumstances not occurred as they did, you and your future spouse may not have come together at all.

Question 7. Do you often finish each other's sentences?

You can get to a point in a relationship when it feels like the two of you are reading from the same script, and it's just wonderful when this happens. This ability to say things simultaneously shows that you've truly connected as soul mates. If this hasn't happened with your fiancé yet, it doesn't mean it can't. If you don't already share hobbies, try to find things that you can do together. Then, once you begin to have similar experiences and attend events together—plus, talk about those shared experiences—you'll begin to speak the same language where finishing each other's sentences is commonplace. This will help get you two thinking along the same lines and, as mentioned previously, help create those similarities in life that ensure your ability to become soul mates.

Wedding Wisdom

To have found someone that I trust, love, and admire and who feels the same way about me is the most beautiful detail of our wedding. Everything else is just extra icing on the cake.

KIMBERLY, NEW YORK

Question 8. When you and your fiancé speak about such things in life as your values, do you feel as if you're speaking in one voice? When you disagree, do you maintain deep mutual respect for each other?

Again, being connected and having similarities is the key to answering this question in the affirmative. If you don't have a shared value system or similar life goals, then you're going to have a hard time forging a spiritual bond and creating a successful marriage.

A recent study—six years in the making—focused on why some couples live happily ever after and others don't. During this study, researchers interviewed recently married couples and asked them a series of questions about their courtship and marriage; the researchers found that newlyweds who were already tuned in to their partner's wants, desires, and thought processes were most likely to stay married. These couples valued their relationships and the bonds that they'd created with their partners. In addition, these couples seemed to speak in one voice and in a manner that was supportive of one another. The other couples, whose marriage seemed less

---

Wedding Wisdom

When my fiancé and I were driving back to college from my meeting his parents for the first time, he pulled the car over on this rural stretch of highway and asked me to get out of the car with him. He then told me that in life you need to stop sometimes, look around, and just enjoy where you are and the person that you're with. He said that with me, he wanted to be able to stop and smell the flowers and realize how lucky he was to be with me. He picked some flowers for me, and I still have them to this day. I think that's a wonderful philosophy to have in a relationship.

JENNY, NEW YORK

likely to survive over time, didn't speak in one voice and had long-term goals that were divergent, not parallel. In fact, when the researchers followed up with these couples six years later, they discovered that they'd predicted with nearly 90 percent accuracy which relationships would endure and which ones would fail.

In addition, you need to realize that disagreeing is as much a part of a relationship as getting along. What's important is *how* you argue. The same study that predicted marriage success also touched on the issue of arguments. The researchers found that, in successful marriages, partners were able to disagree about things without becoming disrespectful of their spouses' opinions on the matter. They could discuss their differences in a way that led to a fair outcome and no hurt feelings. In the less-enduring marriages, the partners became mean-spirited during arguments, and they had a hard time resolving differences.

What this research shows is simple: if you want to become your fiancé's soul mate and lifelong partner, then you've got to make sure that you are on a parallel life course, have a shared value system, and are speaking in one voice. In addition, when you argue (and you will), you must do so in a respectful and loving manner.

Question 9. Have you ever predicted when your fiancé might call or what he may be thinking?

Predicting when your fiancé may need to talk to you or whether he might be in the mood for pizza one night is all about being connected with him on a higher level—and being there for him when he needs you. If this hasn't ever happened to you, don't worry: developing this sixth sense isn't that hard if you really look at how you communicate and interact.

For example, one night your fiancé may tell you that he's having a meeting with his boss the next morning to discuss a new project. If you know that your fiancé likes to talk things through before he meets with his boss or afterward to decompress, you'd probably be safe "predicting" that he'll phone you before or after his meeting, and it will do your relationship a world of good for you to be there for him. Likewise, if your fiancé usually cooks but will be working late on Tuesday, it's probably a good bet that he won't want to cook after a long day at work. So, if you guess that he'll want pizza or take-out food on Tuesday night—and surprise him with it back at his house—you'll probably be on the right track. Again, it's all about truly knowing this person you've decided to spend the rest of your life with—and being there for him when he needs you. Doing so will help you predict his calls or need for support. And, ideally, he'll do the same and be there for you in similar situations.

Question 10. Is your fiancé your best friend?

Before you met your fiancé, you may not have been able to conceive of a man being your best friend. Or perhaps you were one of those women who *always* had male friends. Regardless, the person you've decided to marry has got to be your best friend. He's going to be there during the best and the worst of times, and if you don't have

---

Wedding Wisdom

Over the four-year course of our courtship and engagement, we began to flow together so naturally that we could almost antici-pate each other's thoughts and actions. This merging together onto the same plane of existence is what makes our relationship so solid and so true. We have vastly different interests and hob-bies, and we also have our disagreements, but we are completely in tune with each other. I think that the ability and desire to step into each other's shoes and empathize is what makes us soul mates.

KARISA, CALIFORNIA

a friendship to sustain you through everything that lies ahead, you may have a tough time making your marriage last. Like the other questions in the quiz, this friendship issue stems from similarities and from open communication. If you don't have either of them, then you need to start creating situations where you can nurture both of those qualities in your relationship. Find time to talk to each other, do fun things together as you would with your female friends, and continue to have a good time together as you plan your wedding and your life together. That will ensure that you'll become best friends forever—and, of course, soul mates.

Balance: The Bottom Line

I think I've made it clear that I believe only soul mates should marry, and I feel blessed in having a soul mate for a husband. I hope that in reading this chapter—and taking the "Soul Mate Quiz"—you've determined if you and your fiancé are indeed soul mates or at least figured out what you need to do to become them.

I think what it comes down to is this: fate and friendship play a big part in bringing two people together. Once you've forged a spiritual bond, you must cherish and nurture that bond. Doing so will allow you two to have a long and happy marriage.

CONCLUSION

WE'VE COVERED A lot of ground in this book, and I'm sure you'll cover even more as you plan your wedding. I hope that the preceding pages will help you achieve a sense of balance as you plan your wedding and make your day the special event that you'd always dreamed it would be. I hope that your mind, body, and spirit are in great shape by the time you walk down the aisle—and into your married life.

To help ensure that you get the most out of this book, I'd like to do a quick review on the topics we've covered and how together they make the "Twelve Tenets for Becoming a Balanced Bride." If necessary, make a copy of this page and hang it on the bulletin board over your desk or in your kitchen, or fold it up and keep it with you. That way you can read it at times when you're feeling "unbalanced."

Twelve Tenets for Becoming a Balanced Bride

1. Eat well and treat your body right by feeding it good food.
2. Learn to love your body as it is.
3. Take care of yourself by seeing a doctor for a prewedding health checkup.
4. Get your family plan in place before saying, "I do," including choosing a method of birth control that's right for you.
5. Accept the fact that your sense of self will change once you become someone's wife.
6. Work to avoid family feuds by opening the lines of communication between you, your fiancé, and your respective family members.
7. Take time out of every day to do something nice for yourself.
8. Learn how to balance your job, your family, and your friends so you don't lose your mind, your sense of control, or your balance.
9. Exorcise the demons of your past relationships so that you can enter into your marriage with a clean slate.
10. Discuss today the role religion will play in your family tomorrow.
11. Determine how you can make your wedding ceremony meaningful for both of you.
12. Strengthen the spiritual bond that you have with your fiancé and work to ensure that the two of you will become and remain soul mates forever.

INDEX